# AN EXAM GUIDE TO EUROPEAN HISTORY (1815–1953)

## Martin Roberts

**Oxford University Press**, Walton Street, Oxford OX2 6DP

Oxford   London   Glasgow
New York   Toronto   Melbourne   Auckland
Kuala Lumpur   Singapore   Hong Kong   Tokyo
Delhi   Bombay   Calcutta   Madras   Karachi
Nairobi   Dar es Salaam   Cape Town

and associated companies in
Beirut   Berlin   Ibadan   Mexico City   Nicosia

*Oxford* is a trade mark of Oxford University Press
© Oxford University Press   1983   ISBN 0 19 913274 7

Typeset in Great Britain by
Rowland Phototypesetting Limited
Bury St Edmunds, Suffolk
Printed by William Clowes (Beccles) Limited

# Contents

# List of Maps

# *Introduction*

This book is intended to aid those students actively preparing for GCE 'O' level examinations in Modern European History. Half is devoted to what I hope is an interesting and clear treatment of the major political themes since 1815. The other half is a guide to answering typical 'O' level questions.

Such questions take various shapes and this variety has increased in recent years. Not only may essay questions be set which require either a description or an explanation or an assessment but maps, cartoons, extracts and other 'evidence' material may be included which will test a candidate's historical skills in a number of possible ways. Some GCE Boards also set 'multiple-choice' questions where a candidate has to select the correct answer from four or five possibilities.

As well as providing detailed guidance to answering all these types of questions, further examples from past papers are given at the end of the book.

Revising for examinations can be a soul-destroying business. I hope that this approach keeps your mind alert and removes some of the drudgery.

# Chapter 1 *The Vienna Settlement (1815) and the Congress 'System'*

Between 1793 and 1815 French Revolutionary and Napoleonic armies turned Europe upside-down. To defeat Napoleon needed the combined efforts of the four other major powers of Europe – Britain, Russia, Austria and Prussia. They joined together in the **Quadruple Alliance**. Their victories, first in 1814 then at Waterloo in 1815 after Napoleon's 100-day comeback from Elba, ended the years of violent change when the French had swarmed across Europe removing old-established rulers, shifting boundaries and altering methods of government. The huge task of deciding how the continent should be reorganized rested with the Quadruple Alliance. For eight months their representatives consulted, argued, often bitterly, and finally agreed about Europe's future. Since most of these consultations took place in Vienna, they are usually referred to as the **Congress of Vienna** and the final agreement as the **Vienna Settlement**.

## The Congress of Vienna

The main representatives were strong and fascinating personalities. **Metternich**, foreign minister of the Habsburg Emperor of Austria, was a brilliant negotiator determined to get the best deal for Austria, but convinced also that Europe's future peace depended on the major states of Europe being more or less balanced in strength. Britain's representative was **Lord Castlereagh**, a cold, shy man. Though very different from Metternich personally, he had a clear idea where Britain's main interests lay and, like Metternich, was sure that a balance of power between the major states was essential to the future peace of Europe. The Russian Tsar, **Alexander I**, and the Prussian King, **Frederick William III**, were both present at Vienna and often took part in the negotiations rather than their ministers. Alexander was unbalanced with unrealistic schemes for creating a new more religious Europe. Frederick William was particularly grateful to Alexander, whose armies had freed Prussia from French domination. He supported Russia more than his advisers would have wished. Most interesting in many ways was **Talleyrand**, who represented the new French government of Louis XVIII. Talleyrand is one of History's great survivors. An abbot before the French Revolution, he survived to serve and betray Napoleon. Not only did he end up on the winning side in 1814, he was to do the same again in the Revolution of 1830. At Vienna, France's position was a difficult one and Talleyrand used his cunning and experience most effectively.

In 1814–5 the Quadruple Alliance had three main problems to consider: the future of France, the reshaping of Europe and the achievement of a lasting settlement.

# 1 What was to Happen to France?

The future of France was decided by the *First and Second Treaties of Paris*. The first in 1814 put the old Bourbon dynasty, in the person of Louis XVIII, back on the throne and insisted that the gains made by France in Italy, Germany, the Low Countries and overseas be given up. Otherwise it was lenient. Napoleon's 100 Days made the second treaty necessary in 1815. Not surprisingly it was harsher. The French lost territory on their northern and eastern borders, had to pay damages of 700 million francs and to suffer an army of occupation for three years.

Europe in 1815

## 2 The New Shape of Europe: The Vienna Settlement

The new shape of Europe was the chief concern of the *Vienna Congress*. The final settlement was founded on three principles:

**i) The winners had to make adequate gains** They did. *Britain*, whose interests were mainly commercial, held on to the conquests which her powerful fleet had made in the course of recent wars. These included Heligoland, Malta and the Ionian islands in European waters, and Cape Colony and West Indian islands further afield. With these bases and her huge fleet, Britain was able to dominate world trade for the next half century. *Austria* took the Italian provinces of Lombardy and Venetia, parts of Poland, the Tyrol and Illyria. This meant an increase of population of about five million. *Russia* gained Finland, Bessarabia and much of Poland. Alexander allowed the Poles a constitution and some local rights but this policy was ended by his successor, Tsar Nicholas I. *Prussia* gave up part of Poland but was more than compensated by the Rhineland Provinces and part of Saxony. The most serious disagreement at Vienna concerned Saxony. Eventually the combination of Austria, Britain and France stopped a Russian/Prussian scheme of giving all Saxony to Prussia.

**ii) To shape the boundaries of Europe so that the five Great Powers were more or less balanced** If this could be done, none of them would be likely to go to war on her own, as France had recently done, and the peace of Europe would be more easily kept. The gains already listed were made with this principle in mind. In addition, the Low Countries (Belgium and Holland) were united under the Dutch king to make a stronger state on France's northern border. Similarly, Piedmont, to the south-east of France was strengthened by the addition of Genoa.

**iii) The principle of 'legitimacy'** As long as the first two principles were achieved, the leaders of the Great Powers at Vienna were ready to accept a third, the principle of 'legitimacy'. This term was invented by Talleyrand to mean the restoration to their thrones of the old ruling families of Europe of the era before the French Revolution of 1789. So the *Bourbons* returned, not only to France but to Spain and to the Kingdom of Naples, the *Habsburgs* to the Italian Duchies of Parma, Modena and Tuscany and the *Pope* to rule the Papal States.

The Vienna Settlement has been strongly criticised. An early criticism was that it was a bullying settlement where the Great Powers ruthlessly protected their own interests at the expense of smaller states. The Finns, Poles and Venetians for example were forced, without any kind of consultation, to accept the government of rulers they disliked. The great Italian statesman, Cavour, who master-minded the liberation of his country from the Austrians in 1859, took this criticism a step further. The Vienna settlement, he argued, was fatally weak because it rested 'neither on national interests nor on popular will', which proved to be most powerful forces later in the century.

Nonetheless it would be wrong to label the Vienna peacemakers as stupid reactionaries, attempting vainly to turn back the clock to the good old days of before 1789. After twenty years of war, they were determined to achieve a lasting peace. In this they were as successful as any peacemakers in modern European history. Not for another forty years, until the Crimean War (1854–6), was there another major European war.

They were also determined to prevent revolutionary upheavals. Here they were less successful but the strength of nationalism and the popular will, so obvious to Cavour in the 1850s, was by no means so clear forty years earlier.

### 3 How to Make Sure that the Settlement would Last

The need for a lasting settlement in Europe led to the development of the *Congress 'System'*. The congresses which took place between 1818 and 1822 resulted from the agreement, made by the Quadruple Alliance, to hold periodic meetings to discuss what measures should be taken 'for the repose and prosperity of Nations and for the maintenance of the Peace of Europe.' Almost immediately, serious differences of opinion could be seen within the Alliance. Tsar Alexander put forward his plan to rebuild Europe on Christian principles and to crush revolution wherever it raised its ugly head. He was able to persuade Austria and Prussia to sign this *Holy Alliance*. Britain however would have nothing to do with it. Castlereagh considered Alexander to be mad.

**The Congress of Aix-la-Chapelle, 1818.** The main topic was France. The army of occupation was withdrawn and the Alliance expanded to include France as a fully-fledged member. Britain moves more clearly out of step when Castlereagh successfully opposed Tsar Alexander's aim of using the Alliance to support all existing governments against revolution.

**The Congresses of Troppau, 1820, continued and completed at Laibach, 1821.** The main topic was revolution. In 1819 students in the universities of the German Confederation rioted in favour of German unity. A playwright, called Kotzebue, was murdered because he was believed to be a Russian spy. Metternich reacted swiftly and sharply. He had the *Carlsbad Decrees* passed in 1819 which brought the Press and universities within the Confederation under strict government control. In 1820 there was a military revolt in Spain against the appalling rule of the restored Bourbon, Ferdinand VII. The Spanish colonies declared themselves independent. In Naples another incompetent, restored Bourbon, Ferdinand I, was forced to grant a constitution.

At the Troppau Congress Alexander insisted that the Great Powers must intervene against the revolutionary menace and Russia, Austria and Prussia (the Holy Alliance powers) signed the so-called *Troppau Protocol* by which they claimed the right to intervene, as they saw fit, to prevent revolutionary change. Britain was not represented at Troppau. In a now famous document, the State Paper of 5 May 1820, Castlereagh had already made Britain's attitude clear. The Quadruple Alliance, he argued, had been formed to maintain the general peace of Europe between states. It had not been formed to interfere in the internal affairs of particular states. Such interference was extremely undesirable. Britain's objections were ignored. At Laibach, the Holy Alliance agreed that the Austrian army should go to the aid of Ferdinand I in Naples. He was soon restored to his previous position and a revolt in Piedmont was also crushed.

**The Congress of Verona, 1822.** The main topic was continuing disturbances in Spain. The French government, shocked by the recent murder of the Duc de Berry, nephew of their king, was ready to support the Holy Alliance and take action against revolutionaries. Britain, represented now by the Duke of Wellington, stuck to the position laid down in Castlereagh's State Paper. Once again Britain was ignored. The French marched to the aid of Ferdinand of Spain and by the end of 1823 the Spanish revolt was over.

Britain now decided to withdraw from the congresses. Her new foreign secretary, Canning, worked actively with Monroe, President of the USA, to support the former Spanish colonies in their independence. By the *Monroe Doctrine* of 1823 the USA made it clear that European interference in the New World would not be tolerated and Holy Alliance plans to win the colonies back for Spain had to be abandoned.

The so-called Congress System was over. From now on, the Great Powers looked for allies, depending on the particular situation at the time. For example, the revolt of the Greeks against Turkish rule in 1821 eventually had the Russians, British and French working together with the Greeks against the Turks, and very much against the advice of Metternich. Nonetheless though periodic congresses of the major powers were no longer held, the idea that a concerted effort should be made to act together to maintain peace, that there was in fact a 'Concert of Europe', remained an influential one for many years to come.

## The Main Events

| | |
|---|---|
| 1814 | First defeat of Napoleon. First Treaty of Paris. Vienna Congress begins. |
| 1815 | Second defeat (Waterloo) of Napoleon. Second Treaty of Paris. Vienna Settlement completed. |
| 1818 | Congress of Aix-la-Chapelle. |
| 1818–21 | Revolutionary disturbances in the German Confederation, Piedmont, Naples, Spain, Portugal and the Spanish colonies in South America. |
| 1819 | The Carlsbad Decrees. |
| 1820 | The Congress of Troppau. |
| 1821 | The Congress of Laibach (the continuation of Troppau). Austrian troops crush revolts in Italy. |
| 1822 | Congress of Verona. |
| 1823 | Spanish revolt crushed by French army. Monroe Doctrine. |

## Some Important Terms

| | |
|---|---|
| Quadruple Alliance | Britain, Austria, Prussia and Russia, an alliance to defeat Napoleon. |
| Quintuple Alliance | the Quadruple Alliance plus France from 1818. |
| Holy Alliance | Tsar Alexander II's scheme to keep Europe Christian and anti-revolutionary. Britain was strongly against it from the start but, though Metternich did not take it seriously, Austria and Prussia supported it. |
| Legitimacy | the principle that the ruler of an area before 1789 was the legitimate or rightful ruler of that area in 1815, e.g. the Bourbons in France or in Naples. |
| Liberalism | the political belief that individual freedom matters, especially the freedom to express one's opinions, to act according to one's conscience and to be represented in an elected assembly; also that trade should be free from government interference. |
| Nationalism | the political belief that people sharing a common language, a common history and a clearly-defined geographical area should govern themselves as a nation-state and not be ruled by foreigners. |

9

# Guide to Questions

## Specimen Question 1

Since the Vienna peacemakers made so many changes to the map of Europe, examiners frequently ask map questions. The following is typical. Before you try to answer it, spend a few minutes studying the map on page 6 then, relying on your memory, have a go.

*Study the map (opposite) of Europe after the peace settlement of 1814–15, and then answer questions a) to g) which follow:*

a) Name the political organization bounded by the thick black line (m–m) after 1815. *(1)*

b) Name (i) Empire G shaded in horizontal lines; (ii) its Emperor at the time of the peace settlement of 1814–15; (iii) its leading statesman at that time; (iv) the city of this Empire in which the peace conference of 1814–15 met. *(4)*

c) Name (i) Territories X and Y which were added to Empire G in the peace settlement; (ii) the group of fortresses on the boundary between X and Y which helped to preserve the Emperor's authority in this area. *(3)*

d) Identify clearly, by letter and by name, two independent states shown on this map which could properly be called 'nation-states' at this time. *(2)*

e) Which European ruler took charge of Area E under the terms of the peace settlement of 1814–15, and what arrangements were made for the government of this Area? *(2)*

f) Explain the arrangements made in the peace settlement for Area B. *(2)*

g) Identify the state shaded in diagonal lines and lettered CD. Explain how this state benefited from the terms of the peace settlement of 1814–15, and give reasons why these benefits were obtained. *(6)*

*(Evidence in Question, Watson, Rayner and Stapley)*

The numbers in brackets at the end of each section indicate the marks allocated to the section. With map questions, and indeed any questions with many sections, be as precise as you can and only linger where you know that many marks are allocated. If you cannot remember a particular geographical feature, don't waste time trying to recall it. Note that in this question there is only one mark for a) and 6 for g). When you have finished, compare your answers with those on page 106.

## Specimen Question 2

As well as accurate factual knowledge about the Vienna Settlement, examiners will expect an understanding of its strengths and weaknesses, e.g.:

*What were the merits and defects of the Vienna Settlement 1814–15?* (AEB, 1975)

This is an analytical question. From all your knowledge about the Vienna Settlement you are being asked to select those points firstly which show its strengths (merits) and secondly those which show its weaknesses (defects).

**Suggested essay plan**  Don't rush into your answer. Spend the first five minutes or so making two lists of rough notes, one headed 'merits' the other 'defects'. Then write your opening sentence which points your essay firmly in the direction you want it to go. There should be three main paragraphs:

**1 Strengths of the Settlement**  Get to grips immediately with the guts of the question,

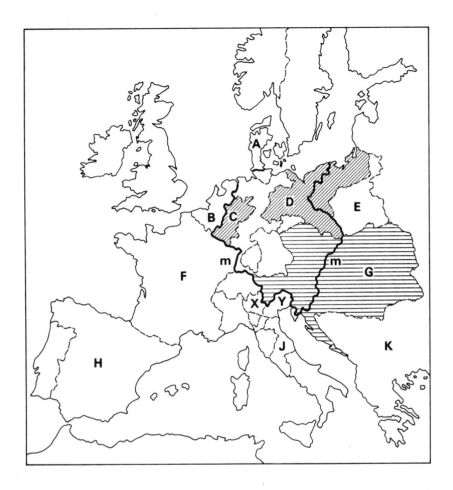

e.g. 'The merits of the Vienna Settlement were considerable . . .' This general point needs to be backed up by particular facts:

a)  no European war again until Crimean War of 1854–6.

b)  France, hitherto the menace of Europe, contained by buffer states – Belgium/Holland, the Prussian Rhineland Provinces, Piedmont and Genoa, and with a 'legitimate' ruler, Louis XVIII ready to co-operate with the other major powers.

c)  the four Great Powers satisfied: **Britain** with overseas gains; **Russia** with Poland, Finland and Bessarabia; **Austria** with extensive Italian territory; **Prussia** with the Rhineland Provinces.

d)  the balance of power maintained.

e)  the idea of a 'Concert of Europe', of the Great Powers making a concerted or combined effort to keep the peace was very much alive.

All this the result of skilful diplomacy, especially by Metternich of Austria, Castlereagh of Britain and Talleyrand of France.

2  *Weaknesses of the Settlement*  Another direct sentence to open this paragraph, e.g. 'The defects, however, were real . . .' Followed by the weaknesses which you have listed in rough:

a) millions of people all over Europe forced to live under rulers whom they hated – Belgians ruled by the Dutch, Italians by the Austrians, the Poles and Finns by the Russians.

b) to France, Spain and Southern Italy were restored members of the Bourbon dynasty who had lost the respect of the majority of their subjects and were never to regain it.

c) since, as Cavour was later to point out, the Vienna Settlement rested 'neither on national interests nor on popular will' it was refusing to recognize some of the most powerful forces of the time; if it kept peace between nations, it encouraged revolutions within them – 1818 to 1821 Spain, Naples, Piedmont and the German Confederation, 1830 Belgium, France and Poland, 1848 all over Europe.

*3 Opinions of historians* Finally your third main paragraph which shows that you are aware that this is a controversial subject to which there is no single right answer: in the mid-nineteenth century, statesmen like Cavour most critical of the Settlement, especially its opposition to national freedom; historians of the late nineteenth and early twentieth century usually agreed with Cavour; with the failure of the peace settlements of 1919 and of 1945, later twentieth-century historians have come to place greater emphasis on the success of the Vienna peacemakers in making a peace between European nations which was to last nearly forty years.

**Specimen Question 3**

An increasing number of examination boards use multiple-choice questions to test parts of their syllabuses. They will give you a question with four or five possible answers, only one of which is correct. When faced with such a question, always study each of the alternatives carefully. Even if you are not absolutely sure of the correct answer immediately, you will often be able to get to it by a process of elimination. Here is an example:

*The last Congress at which all the major powers were represented was held at:*
*A Aix-la-Chapelle in 1818*
*B Troppau in 1820*
*C Verona in 1822*
*D St Petersburg in 1825*     (Cambridge, 1976)

The question asks for **all** the major powers which includes Britain. You know that Britain went to Aix-la-Chapelle, and reluctantly to Verona, though Castlereagh had refused to go to Troppau. Following the Verona Congress, Britain decided to attend no more. So C is the correct answer.

# Chapter 2 *The Eastern Question 1815–85*

The terror of Europe between 1400 and 1700 were the Ottoman Turks. They had conquered Constantinople in 1453. Then they had advanced confidently northwards and eastwards into Europe and, in 1683, had threatened Vienna. However the Austrian capital withstood them and thereafter the Austrians and Russians drove them slowly back towards Constantinople. Nonetheless as you can see from the map on page 14 they still ruled much of South-East Europe in 1815.

Turkish rule in Europe was weak. The ruling dynasty at Constantinople produced no impressive rulers in the nineteenth century. Its armies were shadows of their former glory. Its methods of government were out of date, inefficient and corrupt. Much depended on the local Turkish officials. In Europe their rule was generally unpopular. They were Moslems while their subjects were Christians. They demanded heavy taxes and their subjects were poor. Years of neglect would be interrupted by years of exceptionally cruel repression.

Consequently Turkish rule in Europe was disturbed by many revolts. Some of these were successful and the steady decline in the power of Turkey continued. This decline was of the greatest interest to the Great Powers of Europe who frequently interfered either to assist the revolutionaries or to prop up the government of the Sultan. Russia was an immediate neighbour. Her Tsars wanted to make Constantinople a Russian city and the Black Sea a Russian lake. Austria, another immediate neighbour, while keen to expand her own power down the Danube valley and into the Balkans, was more anxious to prevent Russia gaining too much. France had important trading interests in the Eastern Mediterranean and close links with Egypt, which in 1815 was still a province of the Turkish Empire. Finally Britain had even greater trading interests than France and regarded the Eastern Mediterranean as a vital section of the sea and land route to India, which was the heart of the British Empire. Britain much preferred a weak and friendly Turkish Empire in this area to a strong and hostile Russia.

So the question of what should happen to the declining Turkish Empire – *the Eastern Question* – was one of the most difficult that the Great Powers faced during the nineteenth century. They never really solved it and it was a major cause of World War I in 1914 (see pages 63–5).

## Montenegro and Serbia 1799–1839

Montenegro was a wild, small, mountainous province looking out over the Adriatic Sea. In 1799 King Peter drove the Turks out for good. Five years later in nearby Serbia Black George (Karageorge) tried to do the same. The Serbs were particularly angry since their Orthodox Church had been placed, by the Turks, under Greek control. This first rising failed, though supported by the Russians, but a second, led by Milos Obrenovic in 1815, was more successful. Milos got the Turks to grant Serbia virtual self-government while remaining within the Turkish Empire.

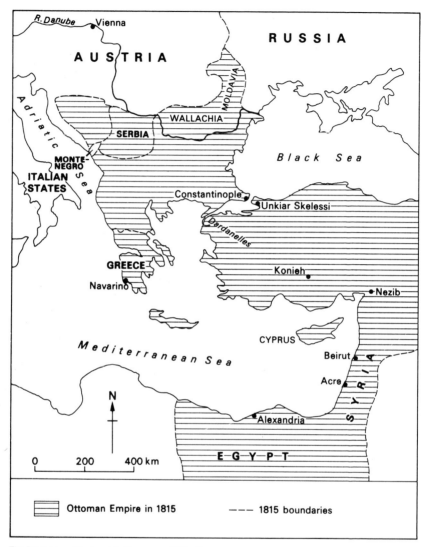

The Balkans and Eastern Mediterranean 1815–41

During the rest of his reign, which lasted until 1839, he extended Serbian territory and improved trade, roads and education. In the meantime, Karageorge had been executed by the Turks having been betrayed to them, probably by Milos. So began an Obrenovic-Karageorgevic feud which was to affect Serbian history for the next century.

# The Struggle for Greek Independence 1821–32

The Greeks too were restless. Some, mainly prosperous and well-educated merchants, formed a National Society (*Hetairia Philike*) the aim of which was to revive the glories of Ancient Greece through the creation of a modern independent Greek nation governed by a freely elected assembly. Others, local chieftains, simply wanted to be rid of the Turks. In 1821 the National Society began a rising in Moldavia led by Prince Ypsilantis. It failed but another in Southern Greece proved tougher. The ideal of Greek Independence caught the imagination of Europe, educated as it was in the heroic history of Ancient Greece. Young men, notably the English poet Byron, came to fight against the Turks. The war proved most cruel. The Greeks massacred the Turks who retaliated by hanging the Greek Patriarch of Constantinople from his palace gates on Easter Sunday 1822. They also killed or sold into slavery the 70,000 inhabitants of the island of Chios.

To begin with, the Great Powers of Europe were reluctant to act. Metternich in particular wished this revolt against the legitimate government of the Turkish Sultan to fail. He feared that Russia would gain from Turkey's increasing weakness. Britain however, moved by Byron's efforts and dramatic death at Missolonghi in 1824, was ready to support the Greeks, as were France and Russia when after 1825 the Turks increased their military efforts against the rebels. By the *Treaty of London*, 1827, Britain, France and Russia agreed to take action. The joint British–French–Russian fleet destroyed the Turkish fleet at Navarino in 1827 and Russian and French troops also attacked the Turks on land. By the Treaty of Adrianople, 1829, the Turks gave control of the mouth of the Danube and a large measure of influence in Moldavia and Wallachia to the Russians. They also agreed to further discussions about the future of Greece. These eventually led to complete *independence for Greece* in 1832, with a German prince, Otto, as the first King of Greece.

# Mehemet Ali 1831–41

Within the Turkish Empire the most able and ambitious ruler was Mehemet Ali of Egypt. He had a good army and, with French backing, a plan to add Syria to Egypt. In 1831 war broke out between him and the Sultan of Turkey, Mahmoud II. Ibrahim, Mehemet Ali's son and leading general, won a crushing victory at Konieh which placed Constantinople at his mercy. In desperation Mahmoud turned to Russia. He signed the *Treaty of Unkiar-Skelessi* (1833) with Tsar Nicholas I by which, in return for Russian military assistance against Mehemet Ali, Turkey would close the Dardanelles to the warships of all other nations. Since the Dardanelles are the straits which link the Black Sea with the Mediterranean, this agreement gave the Russians the control of the Black Sea. Mehemet Ali was now ready for peace. He got more or less what he wanted while the *Russians had won a dominating position* in the area.

Britain was the Great Power most affected by this Russian success. So, when in 1839 another war broke out between Sultan Mahmoud and Mehemet Ali again supported by the French, Palmerston, the British Foreign Secretary, took swift action. Though Ibrahim was again victorious, this time at Nezib, the British fleet went into action bombarding Beirut and Acre and threatening the major Egyptian port of Alexandria. Palmerston also called Russia, Austria and Prussia, but not France, to a conference where it was agreed that Mehemet Ali should be ruler of Egypt and Acre only and that, by the **Straits Convention** of 1841, no foreign warships would be allowed to use the Dardanelles, so preventing the Russian navy from threatening the Eastern Mediterranean. This was a great triumph for Palmerston who succeeded in his policy of propping up the Turkish Empire as a block to Russian expansion. It was also a great humiliation for the French.

## The Crimean War 1854–6

Thirteen years later however, Britain and France were allies fighting together with Turkey against Russia. Trouble had begun in 1850 with a dispute between Catholic priests, backed by the French, and Orthodox priests, backed by the Russians, over their rights as guardians of the Christian **Holy Places** in Jerusalem and Bethlehem. From this trivial start, the Great Powers muddled their way into war. The Russians made the situation more serious by claiming a general right to protect Christians within the Turkish Empire as and when they saw fit. Britain regarded this claim as a disguise to increase Russian influence within the Turkish Empire. The British leaders were divided and public opinion became hysterically anti-Russian. Tsar Nicholas however did not believe that the British seriously meant war and moved troops into Moldavia and Wallachia. The Turks were sure that Britain would fight and declared war on Russia in 1853. In November 1853, the Russian fleet sank some Turkish ships off Sinope. This made British and French public opinion even more wildly anti-Russian and the two countries eventually declared war on Russia in March 1854.

The Crimean War 1854–6

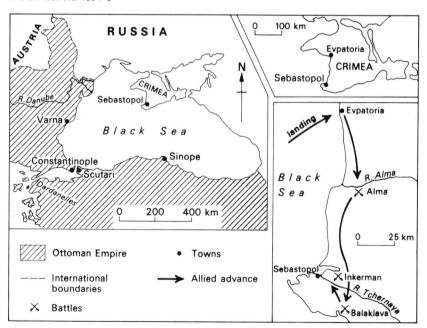

The war brought little credit to any of the armies. The French were competent and Todleben, the Russian commander of the defence of Sebastopol, displayed energy and intelligence. Otherwise the preparations for the war and the leadership during it were appalling. Britain and France intended to fight a limited war to persuade the Russians to withdraw from Turkish territory and give up their claim to protect the Turkish Christians. A small Franco–British force landed at Varna, between Constantinople and the Danube, but since the Austrians would not allow fighting near the mouth of the Danube, the main French and British forces aimed instead to capture the port of Sebastopol on the Crimean peninsula. Hence the war is usually called the Crimean War. Having landed at Evpatoria the first attacks were made so slowly that Todleben had time to improve Sebastopol's defences. An indecisive battle was fought by the River Alma. Eventually the city was surrounded, stormed, and captured.

Before this happened Russian relief forces were driven off after minor battles at Inkerman, Balaklava and the Tchernaya River. It was at Balaklava when the British Light Brigade was virtually destroyed having been sent charging up the wrong valley into the full blast of the main Russian guns. Casualties on both sides were frightful, more from disease than battle wounds. At Scutari Florence Nightingale became famous for her nursing work. British public opinion was also sobered by the reports from W. H. Russell of the Times, one of the first journalists to report direct from the front line of the war. In 1855 not only did Sebastopol fall, but Austria joined the war against Russia and Tsar Nicholas I died. His successor, Alexander II, was ready for peace. By the time the war ended in 1856, half a million men had died making the Crimean War the most costly in European history between 1815 and 1914.

### The Peace of Paris 1856
Britain and France achieved their immediate aims. Russia gave up land at the mouth of the Danube and her claim to protect Turkish Christians. The **Black Sea** was open to merchant ships of all nations during times of peace and closed to all warships. The **Danube** became an international waterway. Though the Turkish government promised **reforms** to improve the situation of its European subjects, its power was further weakened by Serbia and Moldavia–Wallachia being given greater self-government. However, as later events made clear, the Peace of Paris did nothing to solve the Eastern Question in the long term. On the contrary it became more dangerous.

## Further Turkish Decline 1856–85

The Turkish government did not keep its promise to bring about reform and continued efforts were made by the Balkan peoples to increase their freedom.

In 1861 Moldavia and Wallachia united under the rule of Alexander I as the Principality of Romania.

In 1868, in Serbia, Michael Obrenovic caused all Turkish troops to be withdrawn. His assassination continued the Obrenovic–Karageorgevic feud.

The next major Eastern Question crisis occurred in 1875 with the revolt of the provinces of Bosnia and Herzegovina against Turkish rule. They were joined by Montenegro, Serbia and Bulgaria. Sultan Abdul Hamid II attempted, with extreme cruelty, to crush these revolts. Russia then decided that she must come to the aid of her fellow Slavs and declared war on Turkey and advanced on Constantinople. Disraeli, the Prime Minister of Britain, decided to send his fleet to the Dardanelles as a sign of support to the Turks. Despite tough defensive action at Plevna, the Turks were forced to agree to the **Treaty of San Stefano** with Russia in March 1878. An important part of this treaty was the creation in the Balkans of a large new state, **Bulgaria**. Neither Austria nor Britain liked the sight of this 'Big Bulgaria' whose population was mainly Slav and would naturally ally itself to Russia. That same year, a Great Power Congress was held in Berlin with Bismarck, the German Chancellor as chairman. It was a great success for Britain and for Disraeli personally. By the **Treaty of Berlin** (1878), Big Bulgaria was divided into three sections. Only the northern section was self-governing. The middle section, Eastern Rumelia, remained part of the Turkish Empire though it had a Christian Governor-General. The most southerly section remained more fully part of the Turkish Empire. Britain gained the island of Cyprus and Austria–Hungary took over the day to day running of Bosnia and Herzegovina.

Another result of the Treaty of Berlin was the complete independence of Montenegro, Serbia and Romania. Bulgaria, virtually independent, seized Eastern Rumelia in 1885. All that remained to Turkey in Europe were Albania, Macedonia and Southern Bulgaria. But the Treaty of Berlin failed completely to settle the Balkans. None of the Balkan countries were satisfied with what they were given. In particular Serbia felt that Bosnia–Herzegovina should have come to her not Austria; Bulgaria that too many Bulgars were still living under Turkish or Serbian rule and Greece that the Turkish Empire in Europe should have collapsed completely or at worst she should have been given Crete and Epirus.

So the Eastern Question became less what should happen to the Turkish Empire but what should be given to the new Balkan states. Since the Great Powers continued to interfere, it stayed a serious major European problem. In fact it got worse. Serbia and Austria grew more and more hostile and Russia was ready to support Serbia. Furthermore a new Great Power, Imperial Germany, became interested in the area. These continuing Balkan rivalries worsened in the twentieth century and sparked off World War I in the summer of 1914.


## The Main Events

| | |
|---|---|
| 1799–1815 | Revolts against Turkish rule in Serbia and Montenegro. |
| 1821 | First Greek revolts. |
| 1827 | Treaty of London allies Britain, France and Russia. Battle of Navarino. |
| 1829 | Treaty of Adrianople (Russia and Turkey). |
| 1831 | Mehemet Ali and Ibrahim revolt against Sultan Mahmoud. Battle of Konieh. |
| 1832 | Greek independence. |
| 1833 | Treaty of Unkiar–Skelessi (Russia and Turkey). |
| 1839 | Mehemet Ali and Ibrahim in revolt again. Battle of Nezib. |
| 1841 | The Straits Convention (Britain, Russia, Austria, Prussia, Turkey). |

18

| 1850 | The Holy Places dispute. |
|---|---|
| 1853 | War between Turkey and Russia. Battle of Sinope. |
| 1854 | France and Britain declare war on Russia. |
| 1856 | The Peace of Paris. |

## Guide to Questions

### Specimen Question 1

Since the Eastern Question is, like the Vienna Settlement, about land claims and which power won control of where from whom, map questions are frequently asked.

*Examine the map of the Black Sea during the Crimean War and then answer the questions which follow.*

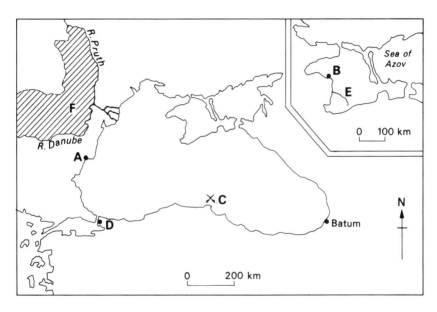

a)   (i) *Name the following places:*
      *Port A*
      *Port B*
      *Battle C*
      *Town D*
      *River E*
      *Territory F*       (3)
  (ii) *What Russian claims against Turkey provoked the war?*       (3)

b)   (i) *What was decided at the Conference of Paris about:*
      *Territory F?*
      *the Black Sea?*
      *the River Danube?*       (6)

(ii) *What other European power contributed to the Allied victory and was represented at the Conference of Paris?* *(2)*

(iii) *Give two different reasons why the peace settlement lasted for so short a time.*

*(6)*

(Oxford, 1975)

Remind yourself of the information in the maps on pages 14 and 16 then see how much of this question you can do relying on your memory. Check where the bulk of the marks are allocated and don't waste time agonizing over particular geographical points. Then compare your answers with those on page 106.

**Specimen Question 2**

Essay questions often ask for a general analysis of the Eastern Question:

*What do you understand by the term 'Eastern Question'? How did the Eastern Question affect relationships between the Great Powers between 1833 and 1856?* (Cambridge, 1978)

**Suggested essay plan** As this question is asked in two distinct parts, make sure that your answer deals distinctly with **both** parts. The first requires a clear and accurate definition of the term, the second which will be longer, is **analytical**. It is asking you to pull out from your knowledge of the facts of the Eastern Question those which made the Great Powers more or less friendly towards each other between the dates given.

*1 Definition* Put into your own words paragraphs 2 and 3 on page 13. That is enough for a definition. The details of the various crises should go into the second analytical section.

*2 Analytical section* For this you should have jotted down some rough notes to get the main crises into the correct order. '**Why 1833?**' you will have asked yourself. Because it was a major stage in the development of the Eastern Question. Greece had finally won her independence from the Turks in 1832, while in 1833 the Russians had won themselves a dominating position over the Turks by the Treaty of Unkiar–Skelessi. **Why 1856?** Because in that year with the Peace of Paris ending the Crimean War, another major stage in the Eastern Question story was completed.

You need two main paragraphs: the first about Mehemet Ali 1833 to 1841, and the second about the Crimean War, causes, events and consequences 1850–6. Outline the main events emphasising the attitudes of the major powers to each other as the events unfolded.

*a) Mehemet Ali* The main points: 1833, Sultan Mahmoud of Turkey faces disaster; threatened by Mehemet Ali and Ibrahim supported by France. Mehemet Ali wins the Unkiar–Skelessi treaty which makes the Black Sea a Russian lake. Relationships between Russia and France and more seriously between Russia and Britain worsened. When the second Mehemet Ali crisis comes in 1839, Palmerston for Britain acts most decisively. 1839 starts like 1833. Mehemet Ali and Ibrahim, with French backing, smash the Sultan's forces, this time at Nezib. The British fleet however bombards Beirut and Acre and threatens Alexandria. Palmerston calls Russia, Austria and Prussia, but not France, to a conference. Result – 1841 Straits Convention. This laid down that the Dardanelles be closed to foreign warships, thus lessening the threat to the Eastern Mediterranean from Russian warships. Mehemet Ali to be limited to Egypt and to Acre. The Straits Convention a triumph for Palmerston, Turkey propped up against Russia, French influence much reduced. The French so humiliated that they briefly considered going to war.

***b) The Crimean War*** Start this section by pointing out the crucial difference between Russia and Britain. Russia sure that the Turkish Empire was bound to decline. The sensible approach for the Great Powers was to decide how best to divide it between themselves. But Britain felt that the Turkish Empire could survive for many years longer if it was effectively propped up: i.e. Britain working with the other Great Powers should oppose Russian mischief-making at the Turk's expense. So Holy Places dispute between Catholic (French backed) and Orthodox (Russian backed) priests leads to Russia claiming the right to intervene to protect all Christians within the Ottoman Empire. Britain moves in to support the French and Turks against the Russians. Clumsy diplomacy generally and aggression by Russia helps bring war. Piedmont-Sardinia joins France and Britain, so eventually does Austria. Appalling incompetence by senior officers and much suffering among ordinary soldiers. Only the French and Todleben, the Russian in charge of the defence of Sebastopol, emerge with credit. Sebastopol falls in 1855, Tsar Nicholas dies and the new Tsar, Alexander II, is ready to make peace. Peace of Paris (1856), Russia ends her claim to protect all Christians within the Turkish Empire; warships, including Russian ones, banned from the Black Sea; the Danube an international waterway. A hard peace on the Russians; before long they meddle again in Turkish affairs. A short-term success for Britain and France; a longer term success for the Piedmontese who joined the war on the side of Britain and France and gained the support of these powers when they sought, in 1859, to weaken Austrian power in Italy. But in the long term, the Eastern Question remains explosive and places such strains on the relationships between the Great Powers that the Balkans become 'the powder-keg of Europe'.

# Chapter 3 *The 1848 Revolutions*

As 1847 changed to 1848 millions of Europeans were more miserable than they could remember. In country districts from Ireland in the west to Russia in the east there was hunger, because potato and grain crops had failed. In the new industrial towns not only did the factory workers face rising food prices, but trading conditions were poor and there was high unemployment. The richer, more educated middle classes were anxious about the economic situation and many of them strongly disliked the existing governments which appeared to them inefficient, out of date and repressive. Among Germans, Italians, and the subject peoples of the Austrian Empire, like the Czechs and Magyars, there was a growing determination to win greater national unity and freedom, by the election of parliaments or assemblies more representative of the people. Such demands were firmly resisted by the existing governments. This combination of widespread economic misery and growing demands for political reform made sure that a revolt in Paris in February 1848 sparked off major revolutions all over Europe.

## Revolution Comes to France

On the evening of 23 February 1848, a noisy Parisian crowd, which was demonstrating against the rule of King Louis Philippe, found its way blocked by soldiers. Arguments turned to violence. The troops fired into the crowd killing about forty. The swiftly spreading news of this tragedy brought revolution to the capital, 1,500 barricades were erected overnight. The next day Louis Philippe abdicated and fled to an English exile.

He had ruled France quite well for eighteen years. Why then did the Parisians want him gone? One reason was *economic*. Like the rest of Europe France was suffering from crop failures and from an industrial depression. This was made worse by a serious financial crisis caused by over-excited investment in railway expansion. A second reason was *Louis Philippe's foreign policy*. He preferred peace to glory and concentrated on staying friends with Britain. In 1846 however, by insisting that his son marry into the Spanish royal family, he lost this friendship. The French however, remembered Napoleon and yearned for success and glory. A third reason was the refusal of his government, led by Guizot, to agree to any major *reforms* even though French industry and society were changing rapidly. In particular Guizot refused to reform the voting system, though out of a population of 35 million only 241,000 had the right to vote. This was the issue that brought the Parisian demonstrators into the streets. Political banquets were held to build up support for parliamentary reform and their success showed how extensive and bitter was the opposition to the government. Louis Philippe made up his mind to dismiss Guizot. He was too late. February 23 and its killings was the following day.

In place of Louis Philippe appeared a Provisional Government which chose itself for the most part, in the offices of two Parisian reforming newspapers. It was unlike any government Europe had seen. Among its leaders were Lamartine, a brilliant poet, Blanc, a socialist political thinker and Martin, a buttonmaker usually known to history as Albert. Though united only by their dislike of Louis Philippe's government they were able to agree to three important decisions in March. Firstly the **National Guard**, which had previously been restricted to men of property, should be open to all classes. Secondly – and this was a scheme dear to Blanc – **National Workshops** should be set up to reduce the problem of unemployment. Thirdly all men over the age of 21 should vote as soon as possible in **elections** to a new assembly. These elections were held in April 1848.

## Revolutions Spread

### The Austrian Empire
By the end of February the news from Paris had electrified Vienna and spread rapidly to the main cities of the Empire. Among the first to take action was **Kossuth**, a clever Hungarian journalist and gifted public speaker, who straightaway demanded a properly elected assembly and other reforms for Hungary. Students in **Vienna** made similar demands for Austria and, backed by rioting workers, threatened the imperial palace and took control of the city. The Emperor Ferdinand I was not equal to the occasion. A stupid man, he was taken by surprise and his government was divided by personal rivalries. Eventually Ferdinand gave way to the demands of the revolutionaries. The hated **Metternich**, who had fought revolutionary movements so successfully for the previous forty years, was sent to an English exile. A new parliament was to be elected by universal manhood suffrage in the western, Austrian, half of the Empire. While this parliament was working out a new constitution, a Committee of Public Safety would maintain law and order and find work for the unemployed. Serfdom, the centuries-old practice which bound millions of peasants to their local lord by forcing them to work some of their time on his land and to give to him some of their produce, was abolished.

In Hungary the main interest of Kossuth and the Magyar majority was to win greater freedom and power for the Magyars. Kossuth was able to get the old Hungarian Diet (or assembly) to agree to the election of a new National Diet. This was based on a wider electorate. It lessened the privileges of the nobility and allowed greater religious and Press freedom. Most important of all it gave the Magyars much greater freedom from Austrian control although they would stay within the Austrian Empire. Since **Budapest**, the capital of Hungary, was in the hands of rioting students and peasants, Ferdinand agreed to these major changes.

The more northerly provinces of Bohemia and Moravia had a mainly Czech-speaking population. There **Palacky**, the Czech leader, followed the Magyar example and demanded greater unity and freedom within the Empire for Bohemia, Moravia and Silesia. He too had the support of the students and workers in the Czech capital of **Prague**. Ferdinand promised the Czechs a charter and a congress was summoned to decide how the Czechs should be governed within the reformed Austrian Empire of the future.

### The Italian Peninsula
Revolutionary ideas were as well-developed in Italy as in any part of Europe. Mazzini's Young Italy revolts may have come to nothing in the 1830s but they had kept Italians aware of the possibility of national unity (see page 37). Political

writers like Balbo and Gioberti, dramatists like Pellico and opera composers like Verdi used their talents to glorify the Italian past and to encourage dreams of a free and united future. Moreover the king of the one independent Italian state, **Charles Albert of Savoy**, was keen to drive the Austrians from northern Italy and was happy to encourage hopes of a national rising, while a new pope, **Pius IX** (Pio Nono) elected in 1846, appeared to be sympathetic to liberal and national feeling.

Not surprisingly 1848 saw revolts throughout the peninsula. In January, revolutionaries in **Palermo** in Sicily forced King Ferdinand II of Naples to promise reforms. News from Paris and, so the story goes, a performance of Verdi's opera *Macbeth*, inspired the **Milanese** to drive the Austrian garrison, after bitter street fighting, from their city. The **Venetians** led by **Manin** persuaded their Austrian garrison to leave peacefully. **Florence** and **Rome** won constitutions from the Duke of Tuscany and the Pope respectively. On 24 March Charles Albert of Savoy declared war on Austria and marched against their aged general in Northern Italy, Radetzky, who had to retreat to the defensive position formed by four fortress towns and known as the Quadrilateral. The end of Austrian rule in Italy seemed in sight.

### The German Confederation

If the news of Paris encouraged the German revolutionaries, they were overjoyed by the fall of Metternich. Of many revolts, the first was in Baden, the most serious in the Prussian capital, **Berlin**. There street fighting between unemployed workers and loyal troops was so savage that the King of Prussia, Frederick William IV, withdrew his troops from the city to avoid further bloodshed. An elected Prussian Assembly met to draw up a new constitution while from all over the German Confederation elected deputies gathered at **Frankfurt** in a *Vorparlament* or Pre-parliament to decide on the shape of the new German nation and how it was to be governed.

## Setbacks and Failures

### In France

The revolution began to run out of steam in the early summer of 1848. The April elections had returned an Assembly which was more moderate than the Provisional Government and which viewed the situation in Paris with alarm. The National Workshops gave two francs per day to anyone for whom work could be found and one franc to those waiting for work. Since there was no pay for the unemployed outside Paris, many of them flooded into the capital and thus made the problem there worse. The Assembly decided that the National Workshops encouraged idleness. It insisted on the dismissal from the Provisional Government of Blanc and Albert and closed down the Workshops. There then followed '*the June Days*' when bitter and starving Parisian workers took to the barricades again, this time against the Assembly. It called in General Cavaignac and 30,000 troops. When the last barricade was finally cleared 1,500 citizens were dead. 6,000 more were sent into exile.

The Assembly then worked out a new constitution. France would be a republic. This *(Second) Republic* should be headed by a President elected by universal manhood suffrage for a four year term of office. The first presidential elections were held in December 1848. None of the revolutionary leaders were elected, nor General Cavaignac who had crushed the Parisian workers in June. The French people voted for law and order and hope for a glorious future, which seemed to them best guaranteed by the Bonaparte name. Their new President was **Louis Napoleon Bonaparte**, nephew of the great Napoleon and otherwise hardly known, since he had spent most of his life in exile.

### In the Austrian Empire

As in France but more so, the revolutionaries began to quarrel among themselves. The abolition of serfdom quietened the peasantry, and improving economic conditions lessened the desperation of agricultural and industrial workers alike. They lost patience with the lengthy constitutional discussions of the more middle-class revolutionaries. More serious still were the racial rivalries that developed. These soon proved fatal to the revolutionary cause.

In Bohemia and Moravia, the Czech-speaking and German-speaking groups quarrelled and **General Windischgratz**, whose wife was killed during revolutionary disturbances, led an Austrian army into Prague and ruthlessly ended the revolution there.

In Hungary the Magyars failed to give to the Slav peoples the same rights that they had won for themselves. Consquently the Croats, a Slav people led by the able **Jellacic**, joined forces with the Austrians against the Magyars. At first the Magyars held their own and Windischgratz and Jellacic turned their forces against the revolutionaries in Vienna. In October 1848 a three-day siege ended the Austrian revolution. Windischgratz saw to it that his tough, extremely conservative brother-in-law, **Schwarzenberg**, became Chief Minister. The incompetent Ferdinand was persuaded to resign and was replaced as Emperor by his young nephew Francis Joseph I. Schwarzenberg then saw to it that all of the 1848 reforms, other than the abolition of serfdom, were cancelled.

In Hungary the Magyar forces inspired by the generalship of **Gorgei** held their own for some months against the Austrian and Croatian forces. In 1849 however Russian troops marched against them as well. Defeated at Temesvar and Vilagos, Gorgei finally surrendered. Kossuth and many of the other revolutionaries fled into exile. Those who stayed were fortunate if they survived the frightful vengeance let loose by the Austrian general, **Haynau**.

### In Italy

In the summer of 1848 the Austrian forces led by **Radetzky** had retreated to the Quadrilateral. Radetzky was 82 but still a fiery and resourceful soldier. He was too good for Charles Albert of Savoy, defeating him totally at Custozza, and later, in 1849, at Novara. Charles Albert abdicated and was replaced by his son Victor Emmanuel II. Custozza was effectively the end of the revolutions in Italy, since without the army of Savoy the revolutionaries had no considerable forces to set against the Austrians and their allies. **Garibaldi** and **Mazzini** set up a republic in Rome which they heroically defended until they were overwhelmed by French forces sent by President Louis Napoleon to win the city back for the Pope. The last Italian city to hold out, Venice, finally surrendered to the Austrians in August 1849.

### In the German Confederation

The longer the deputies at the Frankfurt Parliament discussed what form the new

Germany should take the more divided they became. They talked too much of ideals and principles, not enough of practical matters. In particular they did little to improve economic conditions and their general reputation was seriously harmed when they had to be saved, by Austrian and Prussian troops, from rioting Frankfurt workers.

Meanwile the Prussian government, encouraged by the successes of the Austrians against their revolutionaries took similar action. Though his wife was held hostage in the city, **General Wrangel** marched on Berlin in November 1848 and crushed the revolt.

Back in Frankfurt, the issue which most divided the deputies was whether the new Germany should include German-speaking Austria (the *Grossdeutsch* or Large Germany solution) or should exclude Austria (the *Kleindeutsch* or Small Germany Solution). The *Grossdeutsch* solution would have meant that the new nation would have been dominated by Austria, the *Kleindeutsch* solution, in contrast, would place Prussia in command. Finally in March 1849 it was decided to offer the crown to **Frederick William of Prussia**. He turned it down. He did not believe that the Assembly had any right to make the offer. The crown he said would have been 'a dog-collar fastened round his neck by the sovereign German people'. This refusal was the effective end of the revolutions within the German Confederation though some resistance was continued for a few months more. The deputies of Prussia and Austria withdrew from Frankfurt and before long most of the other deputies followed their example.

### Why did the 1848 Revolutions Fail?

Above all because of the **many differences between the revolutionary groups**. The alliance of industrial workers, peasants, students and middle-class reformers, which achieved such swift success in the spring of 1848, was a temporary one based on the terrible economic conditions of the time. As these conditions improved, in the summer of 1848, the revolutionary determination of industrial and agricultural workers lessened, and the lack of common interests among them and the middle-class lawyers, businessmen and teachers, who took the lead in the various revolutionary governments, became apparent. In the German Confederation, in Italy and above all in the Austrian Empire local **racial rivalries** proved to be fatal to the revolutionary cause.

In comparison once they had recovered from their first surprise the **counter-revolutionary leaders were decisive and ruthless** and they never lost control of the armies. It was the belief of Schwarzenberg that 'bayonets are good for everything except sitting on' and, energetically supported by the likes of Windischgratz, Radetzky, Wrangel and Haynau, he saw to it that revolution was stamped out everywhere, as swiftly and as mercilessly as possible.

The counter-revolutionaries were helped by another cruel and powerful force, the **cholera epidemic of 1848**. This savage, waterborne disease struck the urban populations of Europe especially hard. People haunted by cholera lost much of their keenness to man the revolutionary barricades.

### Were the Revolutions a Total Failure?

Thousands of revolutionaries had been killed, thousands more driven into exile. The old governments were back (Metternich included) and ruled much as before. But not all the efforts were wasted. In Italy Garibaldi's heroism in Rome kept alive hopes of national independence; in many German states, Prussia included, constitutions were granted and parliaments, usually with limited powers only, set up. Above all, in the Austrian Empire serfdom stayed abolished and the lives of millions of peasants became freer and, in the long run, much improved.

## The Main Events

| | |
|---|---|
| 1848 February | Revolution in Paris. |
| March | Revolution spreads to Budapest, Vienna, Prague, Milan, Venice and the German Confederation. |
| | Charles Albert of Piedmont invades Lombardy. |
| April | New Assembly elected in France. Serfdom abolished in Austrian Empire. |
| May | Frankfurt Parliament meets. |
| June | 'June Days' in France. |
| | Windischgratz captures Prague. |
| July | Radetsky defeats the Piedmontese at Custozza. |
| October | Windischgratz recaptures Vienna; Schwarzenberg becomes Austrian Chief Minister. |
| December | Louis Napoleon elected President of France. |
| | Francis Joseph replaces Ferdinand as Austrian Emperor. |
| 1849 Spring | Gorgei and Magyars temporarily victorious, on the battlefield. |
| | Russian Army reinforces the Austrians. |
| | Charles Albert again defeated by Radetzky, this time at Novara. |
| | Frankfurt Parliament offers German crown to King of Prussia, when offer rejected Parliament disbands. |
| August | Gorgei defeated by the Russians at Vilagos. Kossuth flees into exile. |
| | General Haynau takes savage revenge on the Magyars. |

## Some Important Terms

| | |
|---|---|
| Liberal | (see Chapter 1 page 9) |
| National | (see Chapter 1 page 9) |
| Socialist | someone who believes that private property can give the rich too much power over the poor and that important parts of modern industry should be owned by the state for the public good. |
| Conservative | someone who believes that change is seldom for the better and should not be encouraged unless the advantages are clear. |
| Reactionary | an extreme conservative who wishes to turn the clock back to better days past. |
| Serfdom | a relationship in agricultural areas where peasants were so controlled by the local landlord that they had to work on his land as well as on their own and were unable to move from their homes without his permission. |

# Guide to Questions

## Specimen Question 1

An approach popular with examiners is to ask candidates to analyse and evaluate the causes of the failure of the 1848 Revolutions, e.g.

*'The revolutions of 1848 were mainly the work of liberal intellectuals and that explains their failure'. Discuss this statement with reference to the outbreaks of revolution in two countries.* (Oxford and Cambridge, 1979)

Sort out the major issues in rough notes. Questions which immediately spring to mind: What exactly are 'liberal intellectuals'? Were the revolutions **mainly** their work? What is the link between liberal intellectuals and failure? Among the many reasons for the failure of the revolutions was the leadership of liberal intellectuals an important one? And which two countries should be chosen? Knock the complete essay into shape in note form before you begin. It is a difficult one which can easily ramble out of control if you are not careful.

### Suggested essay plan

*Introduction*   Begin with an introduction which shows you know exactly what the examiner is after, e.g. 'Intellectuals are fascinated by ideas, most of which they will have learnt from books rather than from the experience of the world. Liberal intellectuals, intoxicated by ideas about freedom and representative assemblies, played an important part in the revolutions of 1848, especially in France and in the German Confederation. After the failure of the revolutions, it has often been argued that the major reason for failure was too much impractical discussion by these intellectuals, who were incapable of taking decisive action until it was too late. The statement which begins this question reflects such a view. It is however an over-simple one.'

Then use events in France and Germany to show that the statement is too simple.

*1 France*   Liberal intellectuals played their part, e.g. Lamartine and the reforming newspapers, but Blanc though an intellectual was a socialist. The vast majority of workers manning the Parisian barricades were hardly intellectuals. Furthermore the Assembly, which provided the Government of France through the difficult summer of 1848, was made up for the most part of provincial businessmen, lawyers and landowners. Suspicious of major changes it was not liberal nor intellectual. If the French revolution of 1848 was a partial failure, it was because this conservative, middle-class assembly fell out with the Parisian workers and, after the bloodshed of the 'June Days', turned to a strong President to maintain law and order. The French failure was not the result of impractical liberalism.

*2 The German Confederation*   Here liberal intellectuals were extremely active. University students led the first revolts; at *Vorparlament* at Frankfurt, in May 1848, nearly twenty percent of the delegates were professors. This Frankfurt Parliament gave liberal intellectuals a bad name because the delegates did argue for months about the constitution and failed to take active action, while the conservative forces in Austria and Prussia recovered their strength. They also lost the vital support of the workers who had played so important a part in the first success of the revolutions. However, these failures were not simply the responsibility of liberal intellectuals. Many other delegates at Frankfurt were not in the least intellectual. The loss of the support of the workers was more due to the improvement of industrial conditions and tension between employers and employees. Eventually the German revolutions failed because the King of Prussia turned down the offer, from the Frankfurt Parliament, of the German crown. Without Prussian support, the revolutionaries were powerless against the armies still loyal to the kings and princes.

**Specimen Question 2**
Other questions may have a definite geographical focus, e.g.

*List the territories held by the Austrian Empire in 1848. Describe the revolts which took place within that Empire in 1848/9.* (AEB, 1979)

**Suggested essay plan** As long as you know your facts, this is a straightforward question. After a short opening list of territories, all you have to do is to tell the story of the revolutions within the Austrian Empire as accurately and clearly as you can.

*1 The Territories* Those held by the Austrian Empire in 1848 included Austria, Hungary, Bohemia, Moravia, Galicia, Transylvania, Slavonia, Croatia, Lombardy and Venetia.

*2 Describe the revolts* The first risings are in Hungary. Kossuth and the Magyars in Budapest, inspired by the news from Paris, win the establishment of a new, elected National Diet; in Vienna (Austria), Metternich is driven into exile by a movement of students and workers, the Emperor Ferdinand grants a constitution and abolishes serfdom; in Prague, the chief city of the mainly Czech-speaking area, Palacky demands greater freedom from Austrian control; in Lombardy, Italian revolutionaries drive out the Austrian officials while in Venice, Manin persuades them to withdraw peacefully. Faced by Charles Albert of Piedmont's invading army, Radetzky the Austrian general, has to retreat to his Quadrilateral fortifications. So at first the revolutionaries are everywhere successful.

*3 Divisions appear* Czechs quarrel with Germans in Bohemia, Magyars (Kossuth) with Croats (Jellacic) in Hungary, middle classes with workers in the cities. Economic conditions improve. Abolition of serfdom makes peasantry much less discontented. Government ready to fight back. Ferdinand replaced as Emperor by Francis Joseph.

*4 Reaction* Windischgratz successful in Prague; Radetzky defeats the Piedmontese at Custozza and Novara; Windischgratz deals with Vienna. The toughest resistance is from the Magyars and their excellent general Gorgei. Finally in August 1849 the Russians defeat him at Vilagos. Meanwhile Lombardy, Venetia and last of all Rome return to their 1848 owners. The defeat of the revolutionaries, masterminded from Vienna by Schwarzenberg, was thorough and cruel.

# Chapter 4 *Napoleon III*

In December 1848 Frenchmen went to the polls to elect a new President. Lamartine, who had done so much to drive King Louis Philippe into exile and had led the Provisional Government in recent months, got a mere 17,000 votes. General Cavaignac, who had saved the Assembly and crushed the Paris workers during the tragic 'June Days', did rather better with 1,400,000 votes. However, the winner by a large margin, with 5,400,000 votes, was a man who had only just returned to France from exile and was hardly known to the electorate, **Louis Napoleon Bonaparte**. Who was he? And how could he so quickly become the most powerful man in France?

## His Rise to Power 1848–52

### Biographical Details
The new president had been born in 1808 when his uncle Napoleon was Emperor and his father Louis was King of Holland. His parents were not happily married and eventually separated. The young Louis had an unsettled childhood, travelling widely through Europe with his mother, Hortense. He grew up to speak French with a slight German accent. His main interest, in which he had complete confidence, was his Bonaparte destiny and he was soon involved in political adventures. In 1831 he joined a secret society in Italy, the aim of which was to drive from that country the hated Austrians. In 1836 he tried, and failed, to persuade the soldiers in Strasbourg to support a Bonapartist *coup d'état*. In 1840 he tried again this time in Boulogne, and failed again. In 1836, Louis Philippe had simply had him shipped away from France, but he viewed the 1840 attempt more seriously. Louis Napoleon was sentenced to life imprisonment and served six years of this sentence before he made his escape from Ham prison.

At first meeting he was not impressive. Short and inclined to fat, he was not a good speaker either in public or in private. He was lazy and easily bored. He kept his thoughts to himself and usually seemed depressed. However there was more to him than met the eye. He was intelligent and sensitive to the public mood. He had wide interests about which he wrote well. He was a good judge of advisers and his faith in his destiny kept him going through some very bad times.

### His Popularity in 1848
The main reason for his success in the presidential election was **his Bonaparte name**. The French had forgotten the faults and failures of the first Napoleon. They remembered his victories and his reforms and the national glory which his years of triumph had brought. In the later years of the July Monarchy, boring and inglorious years in comparison, the legend was created of Napoleon the people's friend as well as the great soldier. In 1840 his remains were brought back from St Helena and buried with great ceremony in Paris. Bonapartism was a powerful political force and Louis Napoleon knew it. In his writings about his uncle he stressed the points which might impress voters in the 1840s. He also made known his own views about

issues of the time. He wrote for example about the problems of the poor, about canals and about the production of sugar-beet. He presented himself to the voters as a true Bonaparte but living in the present not in the past.

The French peasantry voted for his name and because he seemed to be the best defender of their property. Many workers voted for him because of *his reputation as a social reformer.* The Catholic Church supported him since he offered the least threat to its privileged position. And the more conservative sections of French society voted for him since no monarchist candidate existed.

There was one other reason for Louis Napoleon's success. He had not been involved in the bitter politics of the spring and summer of 1848. The other candidates had. The country wanted *order and calm* above all else. In such a situation this Bonapartist outsider seemed most attractive.

### The Second Republic 1848–52

In the opinion of Thiers, an experienced politician, the new President was 'a noodle whom anyone could twist round his finger'. However it was the noodle who outsmarted the politicians. Despite their fierce opposition, he made himself President for a second term in 1851 and Emperor for life in 1852. This is how he did it. He made sure that he was seen, by extensive tours of the provinces. He pleased Catholics by sending, in 1849, the French army under General Oudinot to guard the Pope against Italian rebels. Meanwhile the Assembly lessened its popularity particularly in Paris by closing down political clubs and by removing from three million working men the right to vote. In 1849 Louis Napoleon felt strong enough to choose his ministers without getting the Assembly's permission. Early in 1851 he dismissed General Changarnier, commander of the National Guard, and the only military leader to whom the Assembly could turn if there came a showdown between it and the President. This showdown came when the Assembly, worried by the President's obvious personal ambitions, refused to agree to a new constitution which would have allowed him to stand for a second term of office. On 2 December, his half-brother, the Duc de Morny, and his Chief of Police, Maupas, organized a swift, ruthless and successful *coup d'état.* There were thousands of arrests and though barricades went up in the Parisian streets they were soon smashed down, with the loss of 200 lives. 'Do you desire the maintenance of Louis Bonaparte's authority?' the French were asked in a plebiscite. 'Yes' said 7,500,000 against 650,000 Noes. Almost a year later, in 1852, another plebiscite asked if the French wanted an Emperor again. The Bonaparte magic was still working strongly. 'Yes' said 7,500,000, 'No' said just 250,000 and 2,000,000 abstained.

## The Second Empire 1852–70

In the first years of the Empire Napoleon's powers were virtually those of a dictator. There was a Senate but its members were appointed by the Emperor. There was also an elected Legislative Body but its powers were limited. In the Departments the key officials were the Prefects who were government appointments and they in turn appointed all the minor officials within their area. Policies were decided by the Emperor, by his strong-willed wife Eugenie and by a handful of able advisers most of whom were relatives or old friends. The press was strictly controlled.

## Domestic Policy

'The Empire means economic progress'. Napoleon III had promised and in this case he kept his word. He was strongly influenced by St-Simon, one of the earliest writers to realize how powerful were the economic and social forces which the industrial revolution was letting loose. The men who really mattered in modern society, St-Simon taught, were no longer kings, dukes, priests and generals but engineers, scientists, bankers and businessmen. Sensible governments would actively encourage such men of the middle classes, rather than the old outdated aristocracy. French industry was in urgent need of such encouragement. Her development was well behind that of Britain and Belgium and she was losing ground to the German states as well.

**Economic progress**   In the next eighteen years this was considerable. Factory workers doubled in number, coal and iron production trebled, foreign trade quadrupled. The main railway network was increased to 12,000 miles (19,300 kilometres) and reorganized on a regional basis by the government. The canal system was also improved.

**Urban development**   This was also a striking feature of the Second Empire. In Paris the energetic Haussmann demolished many old slum areas. In their place came not only broad boulevards and the famous Opera House but excellent sewers, a pure water supply and gas lights.

**Financial methods**   These were greatly improved and made rapid industrial expansion easier. Here the pioneers were the Pereire brothers, whose Credit Mobilier financed much of the railway expansion. Other banks, like the Credit Foncier and Credit Lyonnais, played an important part in this industrial and commercial expansion.

**Freer trade**   This was encouraged by the Emperor and by Chevalier his chief economic adviser. They cut tariffs on many French goods and signed free-trade treaties with a number of their European neighbours. One of the most important of these was the so-called *Cobden-Chevalier Treaty* signed with Britain in 1860.

**Agriculture**   This was not ignored either. Scientific farming, land reclamation and forestry were all encouraged by the government.

**Education**   This was expanded in these years. Duruy, the Minister of Education, was very able. He improved higher education and the training of teachers. He widened the opportunities for girls, modernized the curriculum and lessened the priestly control of French schools.

There was a general improvement in the living standards of most Frenchmen, though certain industries suffered as a consequence of foreign competition or from other circumstances (e.g. the end of cotton supplies to the Normandy textile factories as a result of the American Civil War.)

**Liberalization**   Morny and Haussman had always said that the 1852 constitution did not allow Frenchmen enough freedom. In the 1860s the demand grew for greater freedom. This the Emperor tried to meet without placing his throne in danger. In 1860 he allowed the Senate and Legislative Body a greater say in money matters. In 1863 the Press was allowed greater freedom and the following year trade unions and the right to strike were made legal. However the best days of the Second Empire were past. Morny, the most clever and far-sighted of his advisers, died in 1865 and the Emperor's health was declining. Opposition grew and with it demands for further liberalization. Consequently in 1870 the Emperor agreed to a new constitution, which greatly reduced his personal power and increased that of an elected parliament. A plebiscite gave this new constitution massive approval. It never had a chance to work since it was swept away with the rest of the Empire in the disasters of the Franco-Prussian War.

**Foreign Policy**

*'L'Empire, c'est la paix'* (The Empire means peace) promised Napoleon in 1852. This promise he did not keep. No Bonaparte could stay at peace for long and French troops were frequently in action from 1854 onwards. Generally speaking Napoleon's schemes were quite successful in the 1850s but failed badly after that.

**The Crimean War 1854–6** In the Holy Places dispute, which led to war between Turkey and Russia, Napoleon backed the Catholic interest against the Russian Orthodox Church and so came to fight with Turkey and Britain against Russia. The French army was the only army to show any military competence during the war. The peace negotiations were held in Paris, which brought good publicity to the city and to the Empire. And he got what he wanted for the Holy Places. He had therefore good reason to be pleased with the results of the Crimean War.

**Italian independence 1859** As a young man Napoleon had keenly supported Italian liberals against the Austrians, but despite requests for assistance from *Cavour*, Prime Minister of Piedmont and leader of the movement to drive the Austrians from Italy, he delayed from taking action. Many French Catholics would regard helping the Italian liberals as an attack on the Pope, who was strongly opposed to their plans for Italy. However in 1858 a group of Italians, led by *Orsini*, tried to assassinate the Emperor. They felt that he had betrayed them. Though he had Orsini executed, this attempted assassination spurred Napoleon into action. He signed the secret *Pact of Plombières* with Cavour in 1858 and, honouring this agreement, marched in support of Piedmont in 1859, when the latter had successfully provoked Austria into war. Clear but bloody victories at Magenta and Solferino drove the Austrians from Lombardy. As agreed Piedmont handed over Savoy and Nice to France. Napoleon seemed to have won another great success. Things however turned sour. Worried by his losses and opposition within France, Napoleon double-crossed the Piedmontese and made a separate peace with the Austrians at *Villafranca* (1859). This failed to please the Catholics, shocked many other Frenchmen and gained him a reputation throughout Europe of being untrustworthy.

**The Mexican problem (1861–7)** further harmed his reputation. There *Juarez* had recently set up a republic and refused to pay the debts which the previous government had owed to foreigners. A joint French–Spanish–British campaign was planned to claim these debts but, when Britain and Spain had second thoughts, Napoleon decided not just to continue but to remove the anti-Catholic Juarez and make an Austrian prince, *Maximilian*, King of Mexico. Such a scheme would never have got started if the USA, always the enemy of European adventures in the New World, had not been distracted by civil war. Once this civil war was over, the USA insisted that the French leave. They did, but Maximilian stayed, was captured and executed by a Mexican firing squad. It was a terrible blow to French prestige.

**The Franco–Prussian War 1870–1** brought the Second Empire to an end. Prussia had done very well at the expense of Denmark (1864) and Austria (1866). As a result, Napoleon argued, the balance of power in Europe had been upset and France should be compensated by gains in the Rhineland. His clumsy attempts to bring this about made the South German states more friendly to Prussia. Then came the **Hohenzollern** claim to the Spanish throne and the **Ems telegram** affair (see Chapter 6). The French Press and a group at court led by the Empress were hysterically in favour of war, and a sick Emperor had not the energy to stand against them. France declared war in July 1870. The Emperor led his armies in person. Against him was the brilliant **von Moltke**. The French were out-generalled, out-numbered and out-fought. The Prussians were also better armed. The battle of Gravelotte had the effect of dividing the French armies in two. One, led by Bazaine, took refuge in the fortress town of Metz. The other, commanded by the Emperor and MacMahon, was surrounded at **Sedan** and forced to surrender. Sedan marked the end of the Empire. Paris declared a republic and fought on to final defeat in 1871. The Empress Eugenie fled to an English exile where, after a short imprisonment in Germany, Napoleon joined her. He died in 1873.

The catastrophic end to his empire has tended to hide the achievements of Napoleon III. In industrial and commercial development these were solid.

## The Main Events

| | |
|---|---|
| 1808 | Louis Napoleon born, son of Louis Bonaparte, King of Holland, and Hortense de Beauharnais. |
| 1836 | Attempts a *coup d'état* at Strasbourg. |
| 1840 | Attempts a *coup d'état* at Boulogne. |
| 1846 | Louis Napoleon escapes from prison. |
| 1848 | Spring Revolution. Louis Philippe abdicates. National Workshops set up. Louis Napoleon elected a deputy in the Assembly. |
| | The 'June Days'. |
| | Louis Napoleon elected President. |
| 1849 | French army to Rome to protect the Pope. |
| 1851 | *Coup d'état*. Louis Napoleon proclaimed President for another ten years. |
| 1852 | Louis Napoleon declared the Emperor Napoleon III. |
| 1854–6 | The Crimean War. |
| 1856 | Peace negotiations in Paris. |
| 1858 | Orsini assassination attempt. |
| | Pact of Plombières. |
| 1859 | War in Italy with Austria. Battles of Magenta and Solferino. |
| | Truce of Villafranca. |
| 1860 | Cobden–Chevalier Free-Trade Treaty. |
| 1861–7 | French troops in Mexico. |
| 1867 | Maximilian executed. |
| 1868–70 | Greater 'liberalization'. |
| 1870 | Ems telegram and beginning of Franco–Prussian War. |
| | Sedan. |
| | End of Second Empire. |
| 1871 | Treaty of Frankfurt marks the end of the Franco–Prussian War. |
| 1873 | Louis Napoleon dies in England. |

# Some Important Terms

| | |
|---|---|
| July Monarchy | the period of Louis Philippe's rule from 1830 to 1848 |
| Second Republic | the period from the fall of Louis Philippe's monarchy to the Empire of Napoleon III, i.e. 1848–52 |
| Second Empire | Napoleon III's Empire from 1852 to 1870 |
| The 'June Days' | the violent days in Paris in June 1848, when General Cavaignac led troops against the workers. |
| St-Simonianism | following the ideas of St-Simon and encouraging the leaders of the new industry, the scientists, engineers and businessmen, the productive middle classes rather than the old aristocracy. |
| Liberalization | Napoleon's attempts to give his subjects greater freedom in the 1860s. |

# Guide to Questions

Popular themes are a) the Domestic or Home Policy of Louis Napoleon, b) his Foreign Policy, and c) the 1848 Revolution in France and his Rise to Power.

**Specimen Question 1**

*Describe and assess the domestic achievements of Napoleon III in relation to (i) industry and trade, (ii) communications and (iii) working-class living standards. Why did the Second Empire collapse in 1870?* (London, 1975)

This is a three-part question. It is asking you first to **describe**, secondly to **assess** and thirdly to **give reasons**. As usual, take it part by part.

**Suggested essay plan** 'The domestic achievements of Napoleon III were considerable' would get you off to an efficient start. You could then go straight on to the facts of the description part.

*1 Description   i) Industry and trade*   Doubling factory workers, trebling iron and coal output, quadrupling foreign trade – Pereire brothers, the Credit Mobilier, better banking methods; free-trade treaties, e.g. Cobden–Chevalier (1860). St-Simon's influence.

*ii)   Communications*   Extension of railway network, improvement of canals.

*iii)   Working-class living standards*   General rise in standing of living of population, though some workers in particular industries suffer temporarily from the ending of tariffs. However French industry strengthened by competition, and commerce also got a timely boost. But many French working families live in dreadful conditions still. The lowest rungs of French society gained little from the Empire.

*2 Assessment*   You are being asked to **estimate the value of** these domestic achievements. Two main points: firstly, before the Second Empire, French industrial development was much slower than that of her neighbours. The Second Empire was a period of much-needed acceleration. Secondly, though the Emperor was genuinely interested in these developments and was influenced by St-Simonian ideas, many of these developments would have taken place whatever the government in power. Napoleon's personal achievement should not be exaggerated.

**3 Reasons for the collapse of the Second Empire**   Avoid a long description of the causes of the Franco–Prussian War. You will not have the time, nor is it necessary. The Second Empire collapsed because Napoleon III, against his better judgement, declared war on Prussia and was quickly and completely defeated. Like his uncle, Napoleon's hold on his people's loyalty could not survive defeat on the battlefield. Increasing restlessness with his rule in the 1860s, e.g. demands for liberalization. News of Sedan caused Paris at once to declare a republic.

**Speciment Question 2**

*'My Empire means peace'. How much did Napoleon III do to justify this claim?* (Oxford, 1977)

The short answer to this question is 'Nothing!', but you will need to write more than that! What is required is a description of Napoleon III's foreign policy which stresses how often he was at war rather than at peace.

**Suggested essay plan**   There should be four main paragraphs.

**1 The Crimean War**   (1854–6) The Holy Places dispute, the war in the Crimea (the French army fights well), the Peace of Paris 1856 – success, honour and prestige for France.

**2 Italy 1859**   Sympathy for the Italian liberals, the Orsini Affair 1858, the Pact of Plombières 1858. War 1859, Magenta, Solferino, then the Truce of Villafranca – though Nice and Savoy taken over and victories won against Austria, his separate peace leaves a sour taste and makes enemies inside and outside France.

**3 Mexico 1861–7**   Juarez and the unpaid debts – ambitious scheme to make Maximilian of Austria King of Mexico; French army has little success and is forced out by American threats. Maximilian's capture and death 1867. A bad blow to the prestige both of France and of Napoleon.

**4 Prussia 1866–70**   Bismarck is much too clever for him firstly over the Rhineland and then uses the Ems telegram to provoke him into war over the Hohenzollern candidature to the Spanish throne. The war ends in complete disaster at Sedan and leads to Napoleon's abdication.

# Chapter 5 *The Unification of Italy*

'A geographical expression' was how Metternich contemptuously described Italy. To his way of thinking a single united Italian nation was impossible. If you look at the map of the Italian peninsula between 1815 and 1870 Metternich's attitude becomes understandable. Only Piedmont in the north-west had an Italian ruler. The remainder of the north was ruled either directly by the Austrian Emperor or by his relatives. Across the centre lay the Papal States ruled by the Pope in Rome, while the South and Sicily were ruled by Bourbons, relatives of the ruling family of France. Such divisions had been typical of the peninsula for centuries. To Metternich and many others of his generation they were normal and should continue.

To many Italians, however, unification seemed both desirable and possible. Napoleon had taken control of the whole peninsula and, for a few years, had given it the experience of modern methods of government. The old rulers, restored in 1815 by the Vienna peacemakers, brought back the old corrupt methods and were disliked more than ever. Italians shared a common language and a proud history. The Alps and the sea provided obvious national boundaries. As trade and commerce expanded during the century, especially with the coming of the railways, Italian businessmen came to believe that unification could bring faster economic growth and the domination of Mediterranean trade.

## Nationalist Groups

The main obstacle to unification was Austria and the earliest active nationalists were secret societies determined to drive out the Austrians. Foremost among these were the **Carbonari** (or Charcoal Burners) who took part in the revolts of 1820/1 in Piedmont and Naples and in those of 1831 in Modena and the Papal States. These societies however had no national organization and their impact was only local and temporary.

In 1831 a national movement, Young Italy, was founded by **Giuseppe Mazzini**. Mazzini was an energetic and eloquent idealist. The Italy of which he dreamt was not only united and liberated from the rule of foreigners. It would be a free and democratic republic working with similarly-governed nations to make a better world. Convinced that national unity could be achieved by popular risings, he inspired a number in the 1830s and 1840s. These all failed so swiftly and completely that Mazzini is sometimes written off as an impractical theorist who had little effect on the realities of Italian politics. Mazzini's contribution to Italian unification, however, was very great. The attractiveness of his ideas, which he expressed so well in speeches and writing, and his refusal to accept defeat kept the ideal of a united Italy alive, especially amongst the educated youth.

Enthusiasm for unification increased in the 1840s. As well as the Young Italy movement there were the Neo-Guelfs who wished for a federation of Italian states governed by princes and led by the Pope. This enthusiasm was increased in 1846 by the election of a new Pope, **Pius IX** (Pio Nono) who seemed sympathetic to new

Italy 1815–70

ideas. 1848, the year of revolutions all over Europe, saw numerous nationalist revolts in Italy. Pio Nono proved a great disappointment. He refused to commit himself against the Austrians, and when the Mazzinians set up a republic in Rome he fled from the city in disguise. By now he was a determined enemy of unification and did not return to Rome until the Mazzinians were defeated by the French army in 1849.

In 1848, the best hope of the nationalists was **Charles Albert of Savoy**. He went to war against the Austrians with the slogan '*Italia fara da se*' (Italy will do it by herself). His efforts ended in disaster (see pages 24–5) and by the end of 1849 all nationalist revolts had been crushed. Yet they had not been completely in vain. The heroic defence of Rome against the French by Garibaldi and Mazzini kept future hopes alive.

## Cavour

A clear lesson of the 1840s was that Italy could **not** do it by herself. Liberation would not be achieved by popular revolts alone. Outside help was essential. Camillo Cavour, Prime Minister of Piedmont from 1852, learnt this lesson and acted on it.

More than any single person Cavour was the maker of modern, united Italy. He was most able. Before he became a politician he had made a fortune as a farmer and businessman. At one time or another he held each of the major Piedmont ministries and became so skilful a manager of parliament that he could always be sure of a majority. Victor Emmanuel, King of Piedmont, loathed Cavour personally but was shrewd enough to realize that his political skills were exceptional. Within Piedmont, Cavour supervised some major reforms—of the currency, taxation and customs system for example—and brought about improvements in the railways, overseas commerce and industrial development. He was generally in favour of national unity, but not in an enthusiastic, idealistic, Mazzinian way. His chief interest was to expand the power of Piedmont in Northern Italy and, if national unification was to follow from that, so much the better. Other national leaders, like Mazzini and Garibaldi, distrusted him deeply. In their opinion he was '*piemontissimo*', too interested in Piedmont and not enough in Italy. In fact Cavour was a new breed of politician, realistic rather than idealistic, ready to let ends justify means and to get his way by double-dealing and threats of force.

To whom, Cavour asked himself in 1852, could Piedmont turn in her struggle to drive the Austrians from Northern Italy? France and Britain seemed sympathetic, especially when Piedmont fought beside them against Russia during the **Crimean War** and took part in the **Peace of Paris** in 1856. Neither Great Power was, however, ready to consider active help until 1858 when the French Emperor, **Napoleon III**, survived an assassination attempt by **Orsini**, an Italian nationalist. Orsini believed that Napoleon had betrayed his youthful promises to aid Italian nationalism and his violence, surprisingly enough, persuaded Napoleon to support Piedmont more actively. Later in 1858, at **Plombières** in Eastern France, he met Cavour and they hatched a secret scheme. If Piedmont was able to provoke Austria into war, France would come to her aid. With victory won, Piedmont should gain most of Northern Italy, the boundaries of Central Italy would be redrawn, while the South would be left unchanged. The peninsula would be drawn together in a federation headed by the Pope. In return France should gain Nice and Savoy.

Months passed with Cavour trying desperately, but without success, to provoke the Austrians to war. Napoleon III seemed to be changing his mind. In the nick of time, however, the Austrians lost patience and, by demanding the immediate disarmament of Piedmont, fell into Cavour's trap. War it was in 1859 and the French marched to Piedmont's aid. First at **Magenta**, then at **Solferino**, the Austrians were defeated. Napoleon III by this time had had enough. Shocked by his losses at Solferino and fearing lest the Prussians might joint the Austrians, he hurriedly made peace by the **Truce of Villafranca**, an agreement with the Austrians that Piedmont should have Lombardy but otherwise Italy should remain unchanged. Cavour was beside himself with anger and, when Victor Emmanuel refused to fight on alone, resigned.

Nationalists now took up the running all over Italy. In 1856 **Manin** had founded the **National Society** and, in 1859, its members had led revolts in Tuscany, Parma, Modena and the Romagna. The old rulers were driven out and popularly-elected assemblies voted for unification with Piedmont. Neither France nor Britain was prepared to allow these new assemblies to be crushed. Cavour came back to power in Piedmont and a new agreement was reached. If France were to gain Savoy and Nice, Piedmont could have Tuscany, Modena, Parma and the Romagna as well as Lombardy. This Cavour was prepared to accept, even though Venetia, which had been promised at Plombières, stayed Austrian.

Here Cavour wished to pause to digest the gains which Piedmont had made. But he was not master of events.

## Garibaldi

In May 1860, Garibaldi with barely a thousand young, inexperienced and poorly armed volunteers, whose only uniforms were red flannel shirts, slipped out of the Piedmontese port of Genoa. Their destination was Sicily; their aim to free Sicily and the South from the tyrannical rule of the Bourbons.

Giuseppe Garibaldi was the best-loved hero of Italian unification. Born in Nice in 1807, he first made his living as a sailor but a meeting with Mazzini in 1833 took him into the Young Italy movement. The rest of his life was dedicated to the liberation of Italy. In 1834, as a result of unsuccessful revolutionary activity in Piedmont, he had to go into a South American exile. There he became famous as a skilful and daring guerrilla leader. 1848 found him once again in Italy and his volunteer legion first fought alongside Charles Albert against the Austrian Radetzky and then with Mazzini defending the Roman Republic against the advancing French. So weak were the forces at his disposal that his defence of Rome, though brilliant, was hopeless. With his wife and a few of his volunteers he escaped from the city and sailed away once more into exile, but not before his wife had died from exhaustion, in his arms, on the Adriatic shore. When eventually he was allowed to return to Piedmont, he settled down to the life of a peasant farmer on the tiny island of Caprera.

To his surprise and dismay he found himself cold-shouldered by Cavour and Victor Emmanuel when he hurried to offer his services against the Austrians in 1859. They considered him too simple-minded, too much the popular revolutionary to fit in with their clever schemes of Great Power politics. Garabaldi therefore raised his own forces and fought first alongside the French and then in support of the revolutionaries in Central Italy. He was suspicious of Cavour's aims and methods and bitterly critical of the handing-over of Savoy and Nice (his birthplace) to the French.

Though Cavour tried to stop him, he and his paddle-steamers got through to Sicily. When Bourbon troops barred his way, at Calatafimi, he simply led his thousand redshirts in an apparently suicidal frontal attack and routed them. On his approach Palermo rose in revolt against the Bourbons and within two months the whole of Sicily was his. In August 1860 he crossed into Southern Italy and Bourbon resistance melted away. By September he was in Naples. Cavour however was not pleased. He wanted an Italy dominated by Piedmont not by Mazzinians like Garibaldi. He also feared that Garibaldi might launch an attack on Rome, which might bring the French and Austrians into Italy once more in defence of the Pope and threaten Piedmont's 1859 gains. Cavour therefore persuaded Victor Emmanuel to march south with the Piedmontese army. Papal troops were brushed aside at Castelfidardo and when Garibaldi and the king met, north of Naples, the simple hero was ready to hand over all his conquests to Victor Emmanuel. All the liberated areas voted, by plebiscite, to be united with Piedmont with a **national parliament at Turin**. All Italy was now united, except the city of Rome, which was held for the Pope by the French, and Venetia which was still ruled by the Austrians.

The following years were not happy ones. The Piedmontese ruled the southern provinces harshly. Their northern officials, too often and too openly, lined their own pockets. There were a number of peasant risings. Moreover when Garibaldi tried to liberate Rome with a volunteer force, he was stopped first in 1862 by Victor Emmanuel and again in 1867 by the French. Yet soon all Italy was united, thanks to the Prussians. When in 1866, Austria and Prussia went to war, Italy supported the Prussians. Though the Austrians convincingly defeated both the Italian army and navy, they were overwhelmingly defeated by the Prussians. By the **Peace of Prague**, 1866, Venetia was handed over to Italy. Four years later, Prussia went to war again, this time with France. The French troops defending **Rome** were recalled home and the Italians immediately occupied the city and made it their capital. Pius IX was no readier to co-operate with the nationalists than he had been in 1848. He shut himself up in his Vatican Palace and would have nothing to do with the Italian government, which he declared to be the enemy of the Catholic Church.

## The Main Events

| | |
|---|---|
| 1799–1815 | French rule gives the Italian peninsula a sense of unity. |
| 1815 | The Vienna Settlement brings back the old foreign rulers. |
| 1820s | Carbonari risings. |
| 1831 | Mazzini founds the 'Young Italy' movement. |
| 1830s and 1840s | many attempts at Mazzinian-inspired popular revolts. |
| 1848 | Revolutions in many parts of Italy. |
| | Radetzky defeats Charles Albert at Custozza. |
| 1849 | Roman Republic set up by Mazzini and Garibaldi. |
| | Charles Albert defeated at Novara. |
| | French troops finally capture Rome for the Pope. |
| 1852 | Cavour becomes Prime Minister of Piedmont. |

| 1854–6 | Piedmont fights in the Crimean War with Britain and France. |
| 1858 | Orsini attempts to assassinate Napoleon III. Pact of Plombières. |
| 1859 | War between Piedmont and Austria. French come to Piedmont's aid. Lombardy won for Piedmont. National risings in Parma, Modena, Romagna and Tuscany. |
| 1860 | Garibaldi and the Thousand conquer Sicily and Southern Italy. All the liberated areas vote by plebiscite for union with Piedmont. |
| 1861 | First Italian Parliament at Turin. Death of Cavour. |
| 1866 | Austro–Prussian War. Venetia gained by the Peace of Prague. |
| 1870 | Franco–Prussian War, Rome gained, becomes capital of Italy. |

## Some Important Terms

| *Risorgimento* | an Italian word meaning resurgence or revival which is often used to describe the period when Italian unity was achieved. |
| Sardinia | the correct term for the Kingdom ruled by the House of Savoy which included both Piedmont and the island of Sardinia. |
| The Two Sicilies | the correct name of the Kingdom ruled by the Bourbons which included both Sicily and Southern Italy. |
| Plebiscite | when all voters are asked to vote 'yes' or 'no' in answer to a particular question posed by a government. |
| Republic | a state with a popularly-elected head of state, usually a President. |

## Guide to Questions

**Specimen Question 1**

It is not possible to understand Italian Unification unless you have mastered the basic historical geography of Italy between 1859 and 1871. Remind yourself of the information on the map on page 38 then have a go at this example.

*Examine the map of Italy, 1848–70, and then answer the questions which follow.*

i) *Name the following:*

   *River X*

   *City Y*

   *City Z*                                                *(3)*

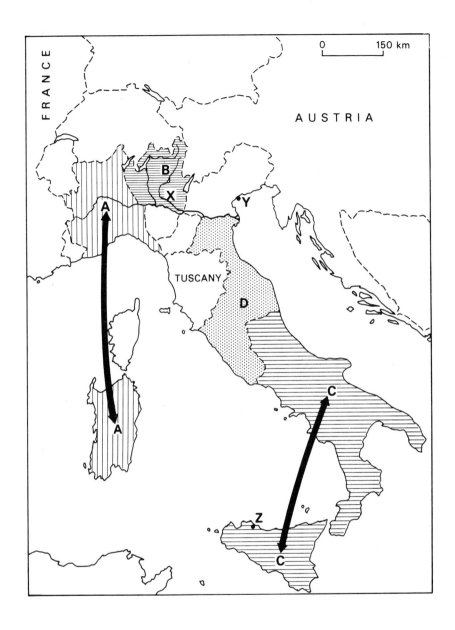

*ii)* Explain when and how *(a)* region B was united with region A (6)

*(b)* region C was united with regions A and B (6)

*iii)* Why did the acquisition of region D present special difficulties? (5)

(Oxford, 1977)

Note how the marks are allocated to the various sections and organize your time appropriately. You will find the answers on page 106.

**Specimen Question 2**

Another approach could be to present you with a relevant quotation from the period and ask you to comment on it, e.g.

*Study the following letter (1860) sent back to Paris from the French ambassador in Turin, and then answer questions a) to f) which follow.*

*Several times in the course of our talk, Cavour raised the possibility of Italian unity, and what he said was this: 'I have always favoured a federal system. You, moreover, have known me long enough to be sure that I have never shrunk from the inevitable outcome of every federation, namely the establishment of a republic. After the armistice of Villafranca, however, federalism was no longer possible. That kind of arrangement was quite impossible, for Italy contained too many differences of temperament. So I came to believe that the only possibility was a unitary state, pure, simple and monarchical.'*

a) *In the first half of the nineteenth century, various suggestions were made for the system of government in a united Italy.*

  (i) *Which Italians most favoured a federal solution? Whom did they wish to be the leader of such a federation?*

  (ii) *What do you understand by the term* federation?

  (iii) *Which Italian leader, before 1850, wrote extensively in support of an Italian Republic?* (5)

b) *In what year were efforts to establish a republic in Rome temporarily successful?* (1)

c) *Between which two belligerent states was the armistice of Villafranca (1859) concluded?* (1)

d) *Explain briefly how these states had come to be involved in a war in Northern Italy in that year.* (4)

e) *What obstacles other than* differences of temperament *stood in the way of Italian unification after 1859?* (3)

f) *Trace briefly the main stages in the unification of Italy, 1860–70.* (6)

(London 1974)

When faced with any source material always read it through most carefully and work out as precisely as you can when it was written, who wrote it and what you would expect his/her attitude to be. With this source we can quickly establish that the letter must have been written after the Truce of Villafranca (see line 5) and the writer is the French representative at the Piedmontese capital of Turin, whose job it was to keep Paris as accurately informed about Cavour's policies as possible. Write your own answers, then compare them with those on page 107.

# Chapter 6 *The Unification of Germany*

The 1848 revolutions had shown German nationalism to be a powerful force. The vital question German nationalists had had to face then, and again in the 1860s, was this: Should Prussia or Austria be the heart of the new nation? The interests of these two Great Powers were too conflicting for them to be united in a larger whole.

## Prussia or Austria?

By 1850, Prussia held many advantages. Economically she was thriving. Between 1818 and 1834 she had created a **Zollverein**, or Customs Union, which bound much of the north and centre of the German Confederation, but not the Austrian Empire, into a single trading unit. Commerce and industry expanded steadily and in the 1840s there was considerable railway building. As economic prosperity increased, so did the number of confident and educated middle-class Prussians, who were keen liberals and nationalists. In contrast, the Austrian Empire remained economically backward, with a large population engaged in peasant agriculture. Social change was slower. The main interest of the government was holding the Empire, with its conflicting racial interests, together. It had no desire to encourage German nationalism, for fear of the effect this might have on other racial groups with national ambitions, e.g. the Hungarians or the Czechs.

The main obstacle to the Prussians bringing about the unification of Germany before 1850 was the attitude of the **Prussian royal family**, the Hohenzollerns. Since the time of Napoleon they had been convinced enemies of revolution and loyal allies of Russia and Austria in their anti-revolutionary policies. In 1849, the Frankfurt Parliament offered Frederick William IV the German crown. He turned it down, believing that to accept such an offer from a popularly elected assembly was like picking the crown out of the gutter. His action marked the effective end of the 1848/9 revolutions in Germany and the old order seemed completely restored. However there were differences. In particular the **relations between Prussia and Austria** had taken a turn for the worse. Their representatives at the Frankfurt Parliament had wrangled over the respective positions of their countries in a future Germany and in 1850 the Prussian king put forward to the German princes (not including the Emperor of Austria) the idea of a **German league** under his leadership. Schwarzenberg, the Austrian Chancellor, did not like the sound of this scheme at all. With characteristic toughness he mobilized 200,000 troops and, at a meeting at **Olmutz**, forced Frederick William IV to abandon his league of princes and to agree to the re-establishment of the German Confederation with Austria as president. Many Prussians never forgave this 'humiliation at Olmutz' and decided that a major struggle with the Austrian Empire was bound to come in time.

### German Liberals

Events in Italy inspired the founding of the **German National Association** in 1859. Its main aim was to hasten the coming of a unified nation. It was liberal since it wished the nation to be governed by an elected parliament and it believed that

Germany 1815–71

Prussia not Austria must be its heart. Now here was a problem which was to bother members of the National Association greatly in the years to come. By no stretch of the imagination could the Prussian government be described as liberal in 1859 and it did not show itself ready to change its ways. Increasingly German liberals had to choose whether or not they were prepared to sacrifice their ideal of a popularly-elected government so that national unity round Prussia could be achieved.

Prussian liberals faced this dilemma acutely in 1862. Prussia did have an elected House of Deputies with real if limited powers and here the liberals were in control. However, since 1857 when King Frederick William IV had had a nervous break-down, final authority rested in the hands of the regent, his brother William. William was a soldier and very conservative. In 1860, with his backing, the Army Minister, von Roon, put forward an ambitious plan of army reform. The liberals disliked von Roon's scheme. It would be too expensive, they argued, and would end the citizen militia which was a useful check on the power of the king. For two years they refused to vote the money needed to finance the army reforms. William, who had become king in 1861, thought of resigning. As a last attempt to get his way he appointed *Otto von Bismarck* as his Minister-President.

## Bismarck

He was the outstanding figure in German history in the nineteenth century. Born into the Prussian Junker (landlord) class in 1815, his basic attitudes were of this class: conservative, religious and deeply loyal to the royal family. After a university education he spent some years first as a civil servant and then as a country squire. Eventually he became a member of the Prussian Diet (or Assembly), where he made a name for himself by his outspoken attacks on liberals and revolutionaries. In the 1850s, at the assembly of the German Confederation, he added to his fame by challenging at every point Austria's leading position within the Confederation. The Prussian government valued him. In 1859 he was sent as ambassador to Russia, and in 1862 as special envoy to Paris. It was from there that he was summoned by William and von Roon to cope with the army-reforms crisis.

Bismarck possessed a lively intelligence, a sharp temper, considerable energy and confidence. He was clear-sighted, cunning and unscrupulous. He believed that his greatest strength was his realism. 'Because they have yet scarcely outgrown the political nursery' he wrote, 'the Germans cannot get used to regarding politics as the art of the possible.' In the real world he had no doubt that the strong always overpowered the weak and consequently he always made sure that strength, which often meant armed force, was on his side. The German word *Realpolitik* (the politics of realism) is often used to describe Bismarck's policies. He was especially critical of German liberals, who seemed to him all talk and no action. German unity would come, he believed, 'not through speeches and majority resolutions, but through blood and iron'. He was determined to bring about a Germany unified round Prussia. This long-term aim he never forgot, whatever immediate problems beset his government. He never risked too much and cleverly outwitted his many opponents.

### Bismarck in Power
His first problem was to overcome the opposition, of the House of Deputies, to raising the money for von Roon's army reforms. His solution was simple, and illegal. He ignored the Deputies and instructed the tax officials to collect the money. Tax officials who showed reluctance to follow Bismarck's instructions were sacked. Though there were protests, the mass of the Prussian people proved

obedient enough to pay the tax demanded and the army reforms were begun.

He now aimed to increase the popularity of his government by pursuing an active and successful foreign policy. In 1863 he helped the Russians put down a revolt in Poland. In Prussia's eastern provinces there were many Poles and Bismarck believed that if the revolt against the Russians had had success similar trouble in these eastern provinces might have followed. He also argued that Russian friendship might prove valuable should Prussia come into conflict in the future with Austria or France.

**Schleswig-Holstein** His first major success in foreign affairs came in 1864. On the northern edge of the German Confederation lay the province of Holstein. Its neighbour, immediately to the north, outside the Confederation, was Schleswig (see map on page 46). Both provinces were ruled, through a variety of historical accidents, by the King of Denmark, though their population was mainly German. One of the many unfulfilled plans of the German liberal revolutionaries of 1848 had been to make both provinces part of their united Germany. In 1863, the new Danish king caused a crisis by declaring Schleswig to be fully part of *Denmark*. His was a rash move since his own claim to the Danish throne was in dispute. Bismarck saw this crisis as a fine opportunity to expand Prussian power in Northern Germany. Claiming to act as champion of the German Confederation, he persuaded Austria to join Prussia in requiring Denmark to restore Schleswig to its former position. When (as Bismarck had expected) the Danish king refused, a joint *Prussian–Austrian* army invaded the disputed provinces. After some hard fighting, which proved the efficiency of the Prussian army, Schleswig-Holstein was conquered.

**War with Austria** Bismarck then used the future of Schleswig-Holstein to provoke Austria. He refused to agree to it becoming a separate state, when Austria would not allow Prussia to have a better trading and military position in north Germany. These differences between the two Great Powers were temporarily patched up by the *Convention of Gastein* (1865) by which Austria ruled Holstein and Prussia Schleswig. In fact Bismarck was preparing for war. He was confident in the strength of the Prussian army. He won more support among Germans by suggesting a thorough reform of the German Confederation along liberal lines. He also gained the neutrality of France by secret discussions with Napoleon III at Biarritz in 1865. We do not know for sure what was said at Biarritz, but it seems likely that Bismarck made some vague promises of French gains in the Rhineland should Prussia overcome Austria.

By 1866, the Austrian government was thoroughly provoked. 'How can one avoid a war when the other side wants it' complained the Emperor Francis Joseph. On 1 June 1866 Austria demanded that the future of Schleswig-Holstein be discussed by the Diet of the Confederation. Prussian troops then moved into Holstein. The Austrians persuaded the Diet to vote in favour of military action and war broke out on 14 June. Nine of the fifteen German states supported Austria. Italy supported Prussia. The general feeling was that it would be a long war and that Austria would win. It was all over in *seven weeks* and Prussia triumphed completely. Under the overall command of *von Moltke* (the Elder), one of the outstanding military thinkers of modern times, the Prussian armies were well-armed and made new and skilful use of railways to shift huge numbers of troops to key positions. On 28 June Austria's Hanoverian allies were smashed at *Langensalza* and on 3 July it was the turn of the main Austrian army at *Sadowa* (Koniggratz).

**North German Confederation**   Austria now lay at Prussia's mercy. King William and his generals were keen to humiliate Austria and enter Vienna in triumph. Bismarck however persuaded them to think again and accept a moderate peace. He argued that a humiliated Austria would prove a bitter enemy and might well team up with France to win back her lost position. Consequently, by the *Treaty of Prague*, Austria lost no land, except Venetia, to Italy. But she lost her dominating position in Germany. The German Confederation was abolished. Prussia made considerable gains at the expense of Austria's allies and dominated a new North German Confederation (see map on page 46). A major step had been taken towards a Germany united round Prussia.

The victories gave Bismarck great popularity within Prussia. Many liberals, who had opposed him over the army reforms, were ready now to support him because of his services towards a united Germany. In the North German Confederation there was a Parliament (*Reichstag*) elected by universal suffrage. Much greater power however was held by the Federal Assembly (*Bundesrat*) whose members were nominated directly by the rulers of the member states of the Confederation.

**Franco–Prussian War**   France had been shocked by the Austrian defeat. The balance of power in Central Europe had shifted dramatically in Prussia's favour. Between 1866 and 1870 Napoleon III tried frantically, but without success, to persuade Prussia to hand over parts of the Rhineland to strengthen France's eastern frontier. The French Emperor was a sick man and French public opinion was excitable. Bismarck skilfully used his opportunities to provoke France further.

In 1870 came a major opportunity. The Queen of Spain, Isabella, was looking for a suitable husband. Leopold of Hohenzollern-Sigmaringen, a relative of the King of Prussia, seemed a possible candidate. The French made it clear however that they would not tolerate an extension of Prussian influence within their southern neighbour, Spain. Bismarck wanted to press ahead with this '*Hohenzollern candidature*' but King William overruled him. Bismarck was depressed. He regarded the withdrawal of the Hohenzollern candidature as 'a humiliation worse than Olmutz'. The French however did not let the matter rest. They sent their ambassador to see King William at Ems and to insist that he guarantee that the Hohenzollern candidature to the Spanish throne would never be renewed. William courteously refused to give such a guarantee and, as was his custom, telegrammed information about the meeting through to Bismarck in Berlin. When Bismarck read the *Ems telegram* he saw that here was a marvellous chance of provoking the excited French into war. He shortened the king's telegram, for publication in the Berlin newspapers, in such a way that the meeting at Ems appeared to have been short and stormy. French public opinion reacted in just the way Bismarck had hoped. Their ambassador and Emperor had been insulted. There must be war. Napoleon III could no longer control events. He allowed himself to be led by a strong war-party within his government. On 19 July 1870, *France declared war*.

Once again the Prussian war machine triumphed, though it had to fight much harder than against Austria. Von Moltke used the railways to gain an advantage in numbers in Lorraine and to separate the main French armies from Paris. One, led by Marshal Bazaine retreated to the fortress-city of *Metz*. The other led by Marshal MacMahon and Napoleon was surrounded and forced to surrender at *Sedan*. Though Sedan was effectively the end of the war, the French fought on for many months. New armies were raised and fought on in the Loire valley until Bazaine surrendered at Metz in October 1870. Paris still refused to give in, though completely surrounded. Her citizens suffered extraordinary hardship until starvation forced their surrender in January 1871.

The Franco–Prussian War ended with the **Treaty of Frankfurt**, 1871. The French paid a high price for their defeat. They lost the provinces of Alsace and Lorraine, rich in iron and textiles. They also had to accept an army of occupation until an indemnity of five billion francs was paid off.

### Germany United

The Franco–Prussian war also marked the final stage in the unification of Germany. As soon as France had declared war, the four independent German states, Baden, Bavaria, Hesse-Darmstadt and Württemburg, allied themselves to Prussia and after the victories of Sedan and Metz, agreed to become part of a united Germany. This Germany was an Empire with the Prussian king as Emperor. On 18 January 1871, in the Hall of Mirrors at the Palace of Versailles, all the German princes acclaimed William as 'imperial and royal majesty'.

Like the North German Confederation, the Empire had its elected *Reichstag* and more powerful *Bundesrat* whose members were nominated by the princes. Since Prussian members were in a majority in the *Bundesrat* and the Emperor kept direct control of the army and civil service, the new Germany was effectively run by the old conservative Prussia.

Any disappointment German liberals may have felt about this aspect of Bismarck's work was far outweighed by their pride in the achievement of a unified nation.


## The Main Events

| | |
|---|---|
| 1834 | *Zollverein* (Customs Union) fully established. |
| 1848–9 | Revolutions all over the Confederation. Frankfurt *Vorparlament.* |
| 1849 | Frederick William IV rejects offer of German crown. |
| 1850 | Treaty of Olmutz between Austria and Prussia. |
| 1861 | William I, having been Regent since 1858, succeeds Frederick William IV as King of Prussia. |
| 1862 | Army-reforms crisis, Bismarck becomes Minister–President of Prussia. |
| 1863 | Prussia aids Russia in the suppression of the revolt in Poland. |
| 1864 | Schleswig–Holstein crisis, war with Denmark. |
| 1865 | Convention of Gastein. |
| 1866 | 'Seven Weeks' War with Austria. Treaty of Prague, establishment of the North German Confederation. |
| 1869 | Spanish Succession crisis, 'the Hohenzollern candidature'. |
| 1870–1 | Franco–Prussian War. |
| 1871 | German Empire proclaimed at Versailles. Treaty of Frankfurt. |

# Guide to Questions

## Specimen Question 1

Map questions are popular so learn the information contained in map on page 46. Other visual evidence is often used, e.g.

*Study this cartoon concerning France in 1870, and then answer questions (a) to (f) which follow:*

VERSAILLES, OCT. 5, 1870.

"The Royal Head-Quarters were transferred here to-day."—*Telegram.*

GHOST OF LOUIS THE FOURTEENTH (*to Ghost of* NAPOLEON THE FIRST). "IS THIS THE END OF '*ALL THE GLORIES?*'"

a) *Which country was represented by the seated figure in the foreground of the cartoon?* (1)

b) *Name (i) the war during which the event to which the cartoonist refers took place; (ii) the ruler whose* Head-Quarters *are referred to in the caption to the cartoon.* (2)

c) *Explain (i) what recent military events led to the situation the cartoonist depicts; (ii) the significance of the map in the hands of the seated figure in the cartoon; (iii) the point the cartoonist makes in his reference to ghostly conversation.* (6)

*d)* *Name the ruler, a relative of one of the ghosts, most recently in power in France. For what reason was he no longer in power?* (2)

*e)* *Taking note of the conversation referred to by the cartoonist, show how far the ruler you have named in **d** achieved outcomes of which the ghosts would have approved in (i) the Crimea, and (ii) Mexico.* (4)

*f)* *How far did the war to which this cartoon refers mark a major change in the balance of power in Europe?* (5)

*(Evidence in Question,* Watson, Rayner & Stapley)

When faced with a cartoon such as this, start by trying to identify the figures. Do not worry if you cannot do so straightaway. Follow up the various clues given in the drawing and in the caption. The most important clues are the date and the map of Paris. Try it yourself then check the answers on page 108.

### Specimen Question 2

*What difficulties faced Bismarck in his attempt to create a German Empire? What advantages did he have? Illustrate your answer by reference to the Prussian Wars against Denmark and against Austria.* (AEB, 1979)

**Suggested essay plan**   This is a difficult question and needs careful planning. Resist the temptation to dash off a general essay on the unification of Germany. Note the four interlocking parts. Your answer should reflect these. They are: 1) Bismarck's difficulties, 2) his advantages, 3) the war with Denmark illustrating these difficulties and advantages, and 4) the war against Austria, again illustrating the advantages and the disadvantages. Rough notes are needed here, e.g.

*1* **Difficulties**   Austrian opposition was the greatest; independent German princes too, e.g. Hanover, Bavaria; distrust of German liberals since 1862; a suspicious Napoleon III lurking in the background.

*2* **Advantages**   Prussia geographically well-placed to dominate Germany, thanks to the *Zollverein* economically dominant too; German nationalism an increasingly powerful force, more in favour of a Prussian-centred rather than an Austrian-centred nation, e.g. the National Association; Bismarck able to use this nationalist enthusiasm to overcome liberal distrust, since most liberals were also ardent nationalists; Prussian army the best-armed and best-led in Europe thanks to von Roon's reforms and von Moltke's outstanding qualities. Bismarck could also count on the solid support of King William I.

*3* **The War against Denmark**   Bismarck able to act as the champion of German nationalism in the dispute over Schleswig and Holstein in 1864. In the war against Denmark the Prussian army proved its efficiency. Prussia's geographical situation also made it possible for Bismarck, in the months following the end of the war, to place difficulties in the way of Austria's administration of Holstein.

*4* **The War against Austria**   Bismarck's success in provoking Austria lost him support in the German Confederation and, when war broke out between Prussia and Austria, the majority of German states fought with Austria. However Bismarck had the support of Italy and the neutrality of France. Starting with the strategic advantage of their position in the centre of the German Confederation, the Prussian armies did the rest. Better-armed (the Dreyse needle gun) better-led, and skilfully using railways to concentrate their numbers in the key strategic areas, they defeated the Hanoverians at Langensalza and the Austrians at Sadowa. Austria also had to send 150,000 troops against the Italians.

# Chapter 7 *Pre-Revolutionary Russia, 1815–1914*

The most backward and reactionary of the Great Powers of Europe in 1815 was Russia. It was also much the largest in area since it stretched from Poland in the west to the banks of the River Amur in the Far East. In 1800, the Russian population numbered about 40 million. By 1848 it had risen to 70 million and continued to grow. Throughout the century the proportion of Russians living in towns rather than in the countryside (1 in 20 in 1848) was less than in other parts of Europe. What industry there was remained for the most part unmechanized. In the rural areas there were two distinct classes; the **nobility** which owned the land and the **serfs** who worked it. Serfdom was close to slavery. A serf could not move from his lord's land without permission. He could be punished as and when his lord saw fit. In most areas in most years he lived close to starvation because his farming methods had hardly changed since the Middle Ages. Consequently violent and frequent serf risings occurred in the first half of the nineteenth century which were ruthlessly crushed by the combined forces of Tsar and nobles.

Since a middle class hardly existed in 1815, the nobility was the ruling class. The local rulers, the army officers, the civil servants of the Tsar, all were nobles. Another important influence was the **Russian Orthodox Church**. For the most part Russian nobles and priests were very conservative. They believed that the **Tsar** was chosen by God to rule and that his word had the force of law. Liberal ideas that questioned his authority and that of church and nobility were not merely wrong, they were evil.

## Alexander I (1801–25)

Since the Tsar held so much personal power, the personality of individual Tsars mattered greatly. Tsar in 1815 was Alexander I, intelligent, sensitive, excitable and unpredictable. Despite a youthful interest in liberal ideas, his chief enthusiasm after 1815 was his **Holy Alliance** which was intended to save Europe from liberalism by the establishment of a new religious approach, supported by the Great Powers. Within Russia he gave increasing power to extreme reactionaries, like Arakcheev and the Archimandrite Photius. On his death in 1825 there was confusion. He had no sons and his two younger brothers, Nicholas and Constantine, each declared the other to be Tsar. In December 1825 young army officers in St Petersburg rose in revolt, in favour of Constantine and liberal reform. Constantine however had no desire to be Tsar, the revolt was badly organized and easily put down.

## Nicholas I (1825–55)

Nonetheless the effect of this 'Decembrist' revolt on the new Tsar, Nicholas I, was to strengthen his reactionary instincts. He trusted no one. Suspicious of the nobility, he employed many German officials. Hating intellectuals whose ideas, he was convinced, poisoned the minds of Russia's youth, he created a huge **secret police force**. It was known as the Third Section and was answerable only to him. Its spies were everywhere, a special watch being kept on writers, journalists and teachers. In 1836 the philosopher Chaadayev was bold (foolish?) enough to openly criticize the Tsar's rule. He was declared insane and forbidden to write any more. Minister of Education from 1833 to 1849 was Count Uvarov. The function of education, he believed, was to make children pious, respectful of the Tsar and proud of Russia. Educational standards, never very high, declined.

Alexander I had allowed some local freedom to the Poles. When Nicholas reduced this, he added to the **Polish bitterness** which eventually burst out in the Revolt of 1830–1. Without foreign assistance, the Poles stood no chance against the Russians. No aid came. Once his army had captured Warsaw, Nicholas placed the country under harsh military rule. Hundreds of Poles were killed, thousands more fled into exile.

Nicholas had an active foreign policy. From 1825 to 1832, he helped the Greeks to win their independence from the Turks. By so doing, he made gains for Russia at Turkey's expense, which he further improved by the **Treaty of Unkiar–Skelessi** of 1833. Though the **Straits Convention** of 1841 (see page 16) was a setback, lands near the Caspian Sea were gained during his reign and the Russian army intervened decisively, in support of the Austrians, to crush the Hungarian revolutions in 1849. In the last years of his reign, he took his country into the disastrous **Crimean War**. Defeats made clear not only the **incompetence** of the Russian generals, but also the **physical weakness** of the under-nourished serf soldiers and the **inadequacy** of the transport system.

## Alexander II (1855–81)

Alexander II quickly agreed to the end of the Crimean War. He was the only Tsar in the nineteenth century who was ready to carry out **major reforms**. After five years preparation, he ordered that serfdom should end in Russia from 1861. 'It is surely better' he told the nobles 'that the reforms should come from above than wait until it abolishes itself from below.' The nobles agreed to this **emancipation** (freeing) of the serfs, partly because of such arguments and partly because they were for the most part generously compensated for their loss of serf labour. The emanicipated serfs had to pay for their freedom within a 49-year period. For those with small plots on the estates of the poorer nobility, this proved a **heavy burden**. Those on the Tsar's wide lands were usually given better holdings and found the compensation payments less difficult to raise. The Edict of Emancipation of 1861 was a great step forward legally for Russia's peasant population, since they could now move about freely and were no longer at the mercy of their landlords. But there was no great economic improvement. This was partly because of compensation payments and partly because a continuing increase in population meant a shortage of land. There were no great improvements in farming methods which were organized as before through the village commune or *mir*. Millions of Russian peasants continued to live close to starvation and had little hope of better times. Peasant risings still occurred.

Another important and more successful reform was the introduction of **zemstvos**, or provincial assemblies. Elected by property owners, they were responsible for local communications, health education and the relief of poverty. The *zemstvos* brought about higher standards of **local** government. In the absence of a national assembly, they gave their members the chance to discuss political matters of more than local importance.

The *judicial* system was also thoroughly reformed during Alexander's reign. New laws of 1864 made equality before the law, trial by jury and the independence of judges basic principles of the Russian system. The old, clumsy system of local courts was simplified, with minor cases being given to justices of the peace. The **army** was reformed too, by an able War Minister, Miliutin.

Alexander was no convinced liberal. He intended his reforms to remedy the weaknesses in Russian society which the Crimean War had brought to light. The Polish revolt of 1863 and an attempt on his life in 1866 made him **more repressive**. Within Russian society there was a group of highly educated intellectuals, full of ideas about the improvement of society but without influence on the government. They are often known as **Narodniks**, or Populists, since they believed a better Russia would develop through the peasant communities. They regarded the village *mir* as the heart of popular life in Russia. In 1873 thousands of young students led a 'to the people' movement, preaching revolution to the peasantry who were more puzzled than excited. After the government had arrested and imprisoned many of the students, the *Narodniks* tended to form secret groups and to attempt assassinations. In 1881, on their eighth attempt, the 'People's Will' group assassinated the Tsar.

## Alexander III (1881–94)

Not surprisingly the new Tsar, Alexander III, was **even more repressive**. Religious, determined and hard-working, he had the assassins of his father hunted down and hung. The secret police was enlarged. A senior official of the Orthodox Church, Pobedonostsev, Procurator of the Holy Synod, became his chief adviser. His Minister of the Interior was an extreme reactionary, Count Tolstoy. Books and newspapers were carefully censored, all ideas for a national assembly were discouraged and the powers of the *zemstvos* lessened.

## Nicholas II (1894–1917)

Nicholas II was to be the last Tsar of Russia. He was as reactionary as his father, but **lacked his determination.** Russia was changing fast. In 1880 the population had reached 97 million, by 1914 it had shot up to 165 million. There was more land hunger and rural misery. Moreover in the 1890s Russia's belated industrial revolution began. Count Witte, an able Minister of Finance, provided government support and attracted foreign investment for key industries like iron, steel, coal and railways. Large factories were built and the number of urban industrial workers increased fast. Much of the profits from this industrial expansion was used by the government to pay for military purposes. Little went, in the form of wages, to the industrial workers. Their conditions were similar to those in other parts of Europe earlier in the century. Their wages were low, their housing and working conditions miserable. Trades unions were banned.

To continue such reactionary policies in such **changing times** was suicidal, but continue them Nicholas did. Underground **revolutionary groups grew** in number and vigour. One important group was the Social Democratic Party, which was founded by Plekhanov and believed in the ideas of Marx. Hounded by the secret police, its leaders spent much of their time in exile. This was the party which Vladimir Ulyanov, later known to the world as Lenin, joined. Another powerful group, with closer links with the peasantry than the Social Democrats, was the Social Revolutionary Party (the successor of the *Narodniks*). They were committed to terrorism and assassinated government officials whenever they could.

Despite these internal problems, Nicholas II pursued an **active foreign policy**. In 1900 Russia joined with Britain, France, Japan and the USA in putting down the Boxer Rising in China. Russian troops then occupied a large area of Manchuria and ignored requests, first from the Chinese and then from the Japanese, that they should leave. The result was the **Russo–Japanese War** of 1904–5. To the surprise of themselves and the world the Russians were humiliatingly defeated. The Japanese fleet attacked the Russian Far East squadron at Port Arthur and the Japanese army invaded Korea and the Liaotung peninsula. The Russian generals were quarrelsome, their soldiers demoralized. After losing a series of battles round Mukden, they had to withdraw from Manchuria. In a desperate attempt to save Port Arthur, which still held out, the Baltic fleet sailed to the Far East round Africa. It was however intercepted by the Japanese fleet, in the Tsushima Straits in May 1905, and annihilated. This crushing naval defeat ended the war; by the Treaty of Portsmouth, Russia agreed to leave Manchuria and to hand over Port Arthur and the Liaotung peninsular to the Japanese.

Within Russia the news of so complete and humiliating a defeat, at the hands of Asiatics, was enough to cause a **revolution**. There had been a severe depression before the war and the Social Revolutionaries' terrorism had reached a new peak. The call-up of peasants for the army reserve disrupted life in the countryside and, towards the end of 1904, liberals in the *zemstvos* were calling for a **national assembly**. The first week of January 1905 saw strikes in St Petersburg, which culminated in a march on the Tsar's Winter Palace. Troops blocked the way and fired on the marchers, killing or wounding hundreds. This '**Bloody Sunday**' was followed by a general strike, which paralysed St Petersburg, Moscow and other cities. Peasant revolts began in February and there was a mutiny on board the battleship *Potemkin*, in Odessa. The Tsar dithered. The Bolsheviks, a section of the Social Democrats who had suffered a bitter split in 1903, set up their first **soviet**, or workers' council, under the leadership of Trotsky in St Petersburg. Strikes, terrorism and rural rioting continued. Finally Nicholas gave in and issued the **October Manifesto**. He promised to call a **Duma** or national assembly and to allow greater freedom to the Press.

These promises were enough to win back to the government the support of liberal reformers and the more radical revolutionaries were too divided to be a real danger. Nicholas however had **no intention of working with the Duma**. As far as he was concerned it could give him advice which he could heed or ignore as he pleased. He certainly was not going to allow it any power. Meanwhile at court the influence of an extraordinary 'holy' man, **Rasputin**, was growing. He was able to control, by hypnosis, the haemophiliac condition of the young heir to the throne and thereby gained a hold over Alexandra, the headstrong and foolish Tsarina. Dominated by his wife and by Rasputin, Nicholas made few good choices of ministers. Only one,

**Stolypin**, displayed energy and drive. Not only did he take effective action against the terrorists, but brought about a major improvement in rural conditions by cancelling the debts still owed by former serfs. His assassination, in 1911, was a disaster for the Russian royal family.

When all available resources should have been concentrated on internal reforms, Nicholas and his advisers decided on an *aggressive foreign policy*. To try to compensate for their setbacks in the Far East they interfered in the Balkans, actively supporting Slav peoples against the rule of the Austrians and the Turks. Military costs rose by more than 200 per cent between 1900 and 1914. Russian policies in the Balkans between 1907 and 1914 helped to bring about World War I (see page 63) which in turn made possible the Russian Revolutions of 1917 (see page 69) and the deaths of Nicholas, his wife and children, the following year.

## The Main Events

| | |
|---|---|
| 1815 | The Vienna Settlement. Alexander I suggests the Holy Alliance. |
| 1815–25 | Alexander I increasingly anti-liberal. |
| 1825 | Death of Alexander I, succeeded by Nicholas I. Decembrist Revolt. |
| 1849 | Russia helps to put down the Hungarian Revolt. |
| 1850–6 | Holy Places Dispute and Crimean War. |
| 1855 | Death of Nicholas I, succeeded by Alexander II. |
| 1861 | Emancipation of Serfs begins the period of reforms. |
| 1863 | Polish revolt put down with Prussian help. |
| 1866–81 | Alexander becomes more repressive. |
| 1881 | Assassination of Alexander II, succeeded by Alexander III. |
| 1892 | Witte appointed Minister of Finance, industrial expansion accelerates. |
| 1894 | Death of Alexander III, succeeded by Nicholas II. |
| 1904–5 | Russo–Japanese War. |
| 1905 | Revolution, from 'Bloody Sunday' in January to the 'October Manifesto'. |
| 1906 | First Duma. |
| 1907 | Second Duma. |
| 1907–11 | Stolypin Prime Minister. |
| 1907–12 | Third Duma. |
| 1907–14 | Russia active in the Balkans. |
| 1914 | Outbreak of World War I. |
| 1917 | Revolutions force abdication of Nicholas II. |
| 1918 | Nicholas II and family killed by Bolsheviks. |

# Guide to Questions

Nineteenth-century Russia is so large a subject that a wide range of questions are possible. Specimen question 1 is concerned with the reign of Nicholas II. Specimen question 2 requires an analysis of Russia's problems over a longer period. The domestic policy of Alexander II is also popular (see Further Questions, page 102).

## Specimen Question 1

*Study this extract from* An Open Letter to the Tsar, *written in 1902 by Tolstoy, and then answer questions (a) to (e) which follow.*

*A third of the whole of Russia lives under emergency legislation, and that means without any lawful guarantees. The armies of the regular police and of the secret police are continuously growing in numbers. The prisons and penal colonies are overcrowded with thousands of convicts and political criminals, among whom the industrial workers are now included. The censorship issues the most meaningless restrictions, as had not even been done in the worst of times in the 1840s. At no previous time have the religious persecutions been so frequent and so cruel as they are today. In all cities and industrial centres soldiers are employed and equipped with live ammunition to be sent against the people. In many places fratricidal blood has already been shed. Yet the strenuous and terrible activity of the government results only in the growing impoverishment of the rural population, of those 100 million souls on whom the power of Russia is founded, and who, in spite of the ever-increasing budgets, or perhaps on account of these increases, are faced with famine which has become a normal condition.*
*(Basic history of modern Russia, H. Kohn, Van Nostrand, Anvil.)*

a) *Name*
   (i) *The Tsar to whom this* Open Letter *was addressed*
   (ii) *the Tsar* in the worst of times in the 1840s. *(2)*
b) *Name the established church in Russia at this time. Which group of people traditionally in nineteenth-century Russia suffered most from* religious persecutions? *(1 + 1)*
c) *In your own words explain the sense in which Tolstoy used* each *of the following phrases:*
   lawful guarantees
   secret police
   fratricidal blood
   100 million souls *(4)*
d) *Suggest reasons why Tolstoy made special mention of* industrial workers. *Why were they* now *significant? (4)*
e) Either *(i) Identify a nineteenth-century Tsar who tried to improve the conditions of the Russian people. Give a brief account of his work.*
   Or *(ii) Explain how and why the resentment of the Russian people against Tsarist rule came to result in revolution in 1905. (8)*
(London, 1976)

With this source question, note the date, which is just before the Revolution of 1905 and the fact that the last section, section (e), is worth 8 marks. Have a go yourself; then check the answers on page 109.

**Specimen Question 2**    *1873*

*Why was there political and social discontent in Russia between 1861 and 1914? In what ways was this discontent expressed?* (Oxford and Cambridge, 1979)

This is a difficult question. It is requiring you to use your knowledge of three reigns, of Alexander II, Alexander III and Nicholas II. You must concentrate on **explaining why** millions of Russians were fed up with the way they were governed in these years and what actions this bitterness caused some of them to take against the government. Use 5–7 minutes making notes to get your ideas into shape.

**Suggested essay plan** *Introduction*    Main reason for discontent the great, and age old, gulf in Russian society between the rulers and the ruled; an all-powerful Tsar, God's chosen ruler, backed by Orthodox Church and nobility, recognizes no limits on his authority; in countryside, nobility in control. A huge peasant class mainly serfs before 1861, living close to starvation, legally and economically oppressed by the nobility; a tiny middle class in the towns have no social standing or political influence. Social changes increase rather than lessen this discontent between 1861 and 1914; growing peasant population causes an acute land shortage by 1900; late but rapid industrialization in the 1890s leads to workers suffering terrible conditions in the industrial towns. A larger and better-educated middle class is less ready to accept its powerless situation.

*1 Reign of Alexander II*    There were reforms; serf emancipation, *zemstvos*, judicial and military, but serf emancipation saddles peasantry with compensation payments and *zemstvos* local not national; in the later years of his reign, Alexander as repressive as his predecessors; strict censorship and secret police.

*2 Reign of Alexander III*    Extreme conservatism following assassination of Alexander II, although Russian society was changing faster than any time in its history.

*3 Reign of Nicholas II*    Extreme conservatism continued, but with less determination; also an aggressive, expensive and disastrous foreign policy. Defeat by Japan 1905 leads to Revolution 1905. Yet Tsar fails to learn from his mistakes. Ignores the Dumas 1906–14, bad influence of Empress and Rasputin; aggressive foreign policy in the Balkans.

*4 In what ways was this discontent expressed?*    By waves of peasant risings in the countryside; by the 'to the people' student movement of 1873; by liberal demands for reforms through the *zemstvos*; by the formation of Marxist revolutionary parties, like the Social Democrats, and by the revolutionary terrorism of the Social Revolutionaries, who by 1900 were murdering government officials by the hundred. Finally in 1905 by a general strike and revolution which disrupted the country for many months.

# Chapter 8 *International Relations and the Origins of World War I, 1871–1914*

Nationalism, always a lively force in the first half of the nineteenth century, became more excitable after 1850. The 'Concert of Europe', the feeling shared by the Great Powers that whatever their differences they had an interest in keeping the peace, dissolved. In 1854 came the Crimean War, in the 1860s the Great Power conflicts which brought first Italy then Germany into existence. Germany was created by the Franco-Prussian War and the seizure of the French provinces of Alsace and Lorraine. The new Germany dominated Central Europe, but feared that a bitter France would always be seeking revenge. European public opinion grew more **fiercely nationalistic**. They gloried in their nation's strength and wished to see it increase. Thus, in international disputes, compromise was regarded as a national dishonour and peace even harder to preserve.

## The Two Camps

### Bismarck's Foreign Policy
Bismarck was the most influential figure in European politics until his resignation in 1890. He considered Germany to be 'a satiated state': to have gained enough. His great fear was that France would recover from the disasters of 1870–1 and, in order to win back Alsace and Lorraine, ally herself with Russia. Germany would then face a dangerous war on two fronts. France's recovery was indeed rapid. She paid off the war indemnity well before the 1874 date agreed and the German army of occupation had to withdraw. France then started rearming. In 1875 Bismarck briefly considered another war against France to end her recovery. However he thought better of this and worked instead to isolate France by a series of alliances.

**The *Dreikaiserbund*, 1873** This was an agreement by the three Emperors, of Germany, Austria–Hungary and Russia, to consult and support each other on matters of international importance. So deep however were the differences between Russia and Austria in the Balkans, that this agreement did not amount to much. The Balkan crisis of 1875–8, which was ended by the Congress of Berlin (see page 18), made these differences clear and caused Bismarck to support Austria more than Russia.

**The Dual Alliance 1879** This followed naturally. It was a much firmer alliance between Germany and Austria–Hungary. Each agreed to aid the other if attacked by Russia and to remain neutral in the event of a war with another power. The Dual Alliance was an important and **dangerous landmark** in the history of modern Europe. It began the forming of alliances which eventually divided the continent into hostile camps armed to the teeth. Since it was a secret alliance, the other Great Powers felt suspicious and threatened.

**Further Bismarckian schemes** The German Chancellor then wove complications into his scheme of alliances. In 1881 the *Dreikaiserbund* was renewed and strength-

N

NORWAY-SWEDEN

*North
Sea*

BRITAIN

DENMARK

*Baltic Sea*

RUSSIA

NETHERLANDS

GERMANY

BELGIUM

L

ALSACE-
LORRAINE

*Atlantic
Ocean*

FRANCE

SWITZERLAND

AUSTRIA-HUNGARY

ROMANIA

SERBIA

*Adriatic Sea*

ITALY

OTTOMAN
EMPIRE

CORSICA
(France)

SPAIN

MONTENEGRO

SARDINIA
(Italy)

*Mediterranean Sea*

GREECE

0    200   400 km

– – – – 1871 boundaries        •••••• French/German boundary before 1870

Europe in 1871

ened. In 1882 the Dual Alliance was converted into the **Triple Alliance** by the
addition of Italy. Then in 1887, after yet another Balkan crisis of 1885–6, he
persuaded Russia to agree to a secret treaty, the so-called '**Reinsurance Treaty**'.
Germany promised, despite her previous promises to Austria, to stay neutral in the
event of an Austrian-Russian war and to support Russian claims in the Balkans.
Russia for her part promised to stay neutral in the event of a Franco–German War.
**Bismarck's fall from power**   A new *Kaiser* (Emperor) had come to the German
throne in 1888—William II. In 1890 he sacked Bismarck and one of his many
reasons for so doing was his belief that Germany's alliances were complicated and
contradictory. The Kaiser was not stupid, but he lacked self-confidence which he
tried to conceal by rash acts and boasts about Germany's power. He and his
advisers failed to agree on what Germany's long-term foreign policy should be and
the Kaiser sometimes went over the heads of his ministers with unpredictable and
dangerous results.

61

The new Kaiser and his minister considered Bismarck to have been too friendly towards Russia. They did not believe the alliance between France and Russia, which had so worried Bismarck, to be at all likely. They therefore ended the Reinsurance Treaty. Bismarck proved to be correct. In 1893, **France and Russia became allies**. If attacked by a third party (e.g. Germany) they promised to come to each other's aid. French money flowed into Russia to finance her industrialization. Meanwhile, **Britain** was feeling the **need for allies**. Previously confident in her industrial strength and in the might of her navy, she had preferred to stay 'splendidly isolated' from the continent of Europe. In the 1890s, however, she had been overtaken economically by the USA and by Germany. She was losing her influence in the Eastern Mediterranean. In 1898 she had nearly come to war with France because of rivalry for the control of the Upper Nile and, from 1899 to 1902, had fought the Boer War in South Africa, aware of the strong disapproval of most of Europe.

### The Formation of the Ententes

As Britain looked for European allies, Germany appeared to be her most dangerous enemy. The Kaiser had been the most outspoken of Britain's Boer War critics and obviously envied Britain's huge colonial empire. Like most Germans he was convinced that Germany deserved a much larger overseas empire, 'a place in the sun' in proportion to her political and economic strength. He also supported his dynamic naval chief, Admiral von Tirpitz, who was building a new fleet designed specifically to challenge the Royal Navy. This navy policy, made effective by the Navy Laws of 1898 and 1900, threatened Britain's island security and independence and pushed her towards closer links with France. Delcassé, the French Foreign Minister, greatly favoured an Anglo-French alliance and King Edward VII made a highly successful visit to Paris in 1903, which paved the way to the signing of the **Entente Cordiale** of 1904. This *entente* was, as its French name shows, a 'friendly agreement' rather than a formal alliance and, in 1904, was mainly concerned with colonial matters in Africa and the Far East. It indicated however a new readiness of these major powers to co-operate. Three years later, Britain arrived at a similar *entente*, or understanding, with Russia. Both Russia and Britain were concerned by the increase in German influence in the Middle East and, following their victory over Russia in 1904–5, expansion by the Japanese in the Far East. Consequently the **Anglo–Russian Entente** of 1907 was chiefly concerned with Asian affairs but, like the Anglo–French Entente of 1904, showed a new readiness to co-operate in the face of German threats. Thus from 1907 the **Triple Alliance** of Germany, Austro–Hungary and Italy was balanced by the **Triple Entente** of France, Russia and Britain.

## The Drift to War 1905–14

These two alliances (the Triple Alliance and the Triple Entente) grew more hostile and better armed. Two areas in particular worsened their rivalry.

### Morocco (in North Africa)

Here Germany was keen to increase her colonial and trading interests. In the great period of European empire-building, Britain and France had done very well,

Germany less so. By their 1904 Entente Britain and France had agreed that Morocco should be a French sphere of influence. In 1905, however, the Kaiser visited nearby Tangier and in a threatening speech criticized the Anglo–French agreement and promised to support the independence of the Sultan of Morocco. A major international crisis followed in which the Kaiser and his advisers, undecided as to what exactly they wanted, were not strong enough to overcome the determined and united stand of Britain and France. By the *Algeciras Conference* of 1906, Germans suffered a major diplomatic defeat since French influence in Morocco was only slightly lessened. The Germans were angered by, what seemed to them, an Anglo–French conspiracy to prevent their winning their rightful 'place in the sun', while for their part the British and French governments decided that their military leaders should prepare joint plans for a war against Germany.

The second major Moroccan crisis blew up in 1911. Because of internal disorders in Fez, the capital, the French sent troops to protect foreign residents. Claiming that the French had broken the Algeciras agreement, the Germans sent the gunboat *Panther* to the southern port of Agadir. As in 1905, the German government was unclear about its aims and the British backed the French wholeheartedly. Eventually the Germans had to back off with the face-saving gain of some wasteland in the French Congo. The *Agadir crisis* caused great bitterness and solved nothing. Convinced now that Germany was very dangerous and a major European war increasingly likely, the French fleet was concentrated in the Mediterranean to deal with the Austrians and Italians, while Britain undertook responsibility for the North Sea.

### The Balkans

These were even more explosive. The Turkish Empire in Europe continued to decay and the Slav peoples within it, like the Serbs and Bulgars, wished to increase their power at the expense of the Turks and each other. Moreover there were many Slavs within the Austrian Empire to the north, who wished to be united to their southern brothers. This the Austrian government refused to consider. It believed that, since the Empire was made up of so many subject peoples, to allow independence to any one of them would cause its complete collapse. Russia was also keen to gain land from Turkey and to support the Balkan Slavs against Turkey and Austria.

**The crisis of 1908**   By the Berlin Settlement of 1878, Bosnia and Herzegovina, though in name still part of the Turkish Empire, were to be administered by Austria-Hungary. In 1908, Austria took complete control of them. The Russians were angry, so too were the Serbians who regarded the two provinces as rightly theirs. Izvolsky, the Russian Foreign Minister was particularly angry, since he claimed that the Austrians had double-crossed him. For a moment war seemed likely, but while Germany promised Austria support, Britain looked for a compromise. In the end Serbia and Russia had to give way. Bosnia and Herzegovina stayed part of the Austrian Empire and Izvolsky set about gaining his revenge.

**The Balkan Wars 1912–13**   These were part of a train of events which began in 1911 when the Italians seized Tripoli in North Africa from the Turks. Fearing that Austria–Hungary would take advantage of the obvious weakness of Turkey and try to take what was left of Turkey in Europe, Bulgaria, Serbia, Montenegro and Greece formed the *Balkan League* and attacked Turkey themselves. In 1912 they drove the Turks back almost to Constantinople but could not agree on how to

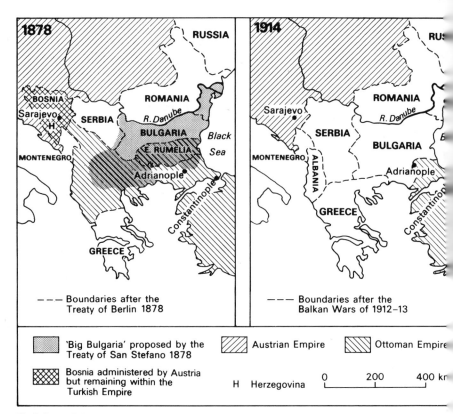

1878 — Boundaries after the Treaty of Berlin 1878

1914 — Boundaries after the Balkan Wars of 1912–13

'Big Bulgaria' proposed by the Treaty of San Stefano 1878

Bosnia administered by Austria but remaining within the Turkish Empire

Austrian Empire

Ottoman Empire

H   Herzegovina

0      200      400 km

The Balkans 1878–1914

divide up their conquests. A new state, **Albania**, was created and the Great Powers interfered to prevent Serbia gaining an Adriatic coastline. They compensated Serbia instead with land which the Bulgars wanted. Another Balkan War followed in 1913 when Bulgaria attacked Serbia who, supported by Greece, Montenegro, Romania and Turkey, was quickly victorious. **Serbia** made further gains in the Balkans and, brimming with confidence, saw herself as the champion of South Slavs everywhere. 'The first round is ours' declared the Serbian Prime Minister Pasic, 'now we must prepare for the next, against Austria.'

These crises deepened the suspicions and rivalries between the Triple Alliance and the Triple Entente. The arms race accelerated. Particularly expensive was the **naval race** between Britain and Germany. In 1906 the tough British Admiral of the Fleet, Fisher, had tried to win the race once and for all by having built the *Dreadnought* class of battleship. The Dreadnoughts were faster and better armoured with more powerful guns than any ship afloat. The Germans however did not give up. On the contrary, they spent more time and money on building their own *Dreadnought* equivalents. There was also heavy spending on the armies of Europe. In 1913, for example, the French began army reforms which were intended to bring their army to a new level of readiness and efficiency by 1916.

**1914**   On 28 June 1914, Archduke Ferdinand, heir to the Austrian throne, was murdered while visiting the Bosnian city of **Sarajevo**. His assassin was a Bosnian student, Princip, who had been assisted by the Serbian secret service. The Austrian government made sure of German support and sent so tough an ultimatum to Serbia that it was clearly bent on war. Though Serbia was ready to agree to most of the ultimatum Austria nonetheless declared war on Serbia. Russia, however, was not prepared to leave Serbia in the lurch, but her Tsar and generals faced an agonizing decision. If they concentrated their troops against Austria alone, might they not be dangerously exposed to a later attack from Germany? Most generals were then convinced that the war would be won by those nations which were able to concentrate their armies in the strategically vital spots fastest and in the greatest numbers. 'Mobilization', the movement of troops before the declaration of war, was vitally important. Tsar Nicholas ordered a *general mobilization* towards both the Austrian and German borders. Kaiser William and his generals now faced a dilemma. They were sure that they would have to fight Russia but the only plan they had was the *Schlieffen Plan* which had been drawn up in 1905. The only way to be sure of final victory, Schlieffen had decided, was to defeat France first and only then undertake the main attack on Russia. As the German generals started the mobilization which would put the Schlieffen Plan into effect, the German government learnt that Britain was likely to come to France's aid. For a brief moment the Kaiser tried to halt the attack on France. However von Moltke, his Army Chief of Staff, pointed out that to do so would both throw his plans of attack into chaos and give the French and Russians the chance of an effective counter-attack. So the Schlieffen Plan was put rapidly into effect. Germany declared war on Russia on 1 August and on France and Belgium, through whose lands the attack on France was going, on 3 August. The attack on Belgium caused a hitherto undecided Britain to declare war on Germany on 4 August.

**The Causes of World War I**

These have proved a controversial subject among historians. Immediately after 1918 blame was placed firmly on the shoulders of the defeated Austrian and German Empires. In contrast, later historians emphasized the explosive nature of the Balkans, the belligerent nationalism which was widespread throughout the continent before 1914, the arms race and the aggressive military thinking which encouraged the approach that, since war was bound to come sooner or later, one should get one's attack in first. They were less ready to single out the Germans and Austrians for particular blame. In the 1960s however, the German historian Fischer swung the pendulum back. From his close study of Germany's war aims he has argued that many Germans were determined to dominate Europe, that military expenditure was increased for this reason and that German generals and admirals carried much greater political weight than in other countries. In Fischer's view Germany must carry the main responsibility for the outbreak of a general European war in 1914, even though the first explosion was in the Balkans. The controversy continues.

## The Main Events

| | |
|---|---|
| 1871 | Franco–Prussian War ends. France loses Alsace and Lorraine. |
| 1873 | *Dreikaiserbund* (League of the Three Emperors) of Germany, Austria, Russia. |

| 1875–8 | Balkan crisis ended by the Congress of Berlin. |
|--------|-----------------------------------------------|
| 1879 | Dual Alliance of Germany and Austria. |
| 1881 | Renewal of the *Dreikaiserbund*. |
| | France conquers Tunisia. |
| 1882 | Triple Alliance. Italy joins the Dual Alliance of Germany and Austria. |
| 1887 | Reinsurance Treaty of Germany with Russia. |
| 1890 | Kaiser William II sacks Bismarck; Reinsurance Treaty lapses. |
| 1893 | Dual Alliance of France with Russia. |
| 1898–1900 | Naval Laws begin massive German naval building programme. |
| 1904 | *Entente Cordiale* (France and Britain). |
| 1905 | First Moroccan crisis (the Kaiser in Tangier). |
| 1906 | Britain begins *Dreadnought* battleship building. |
| 1907 | Triple Entente of Britain, France and Russia. |
| 1908 | Austria annexes Bosnia and Herzegovina. |
| 1911 | Second Moroccan crisis; German gunboat *Panther* to Agadir. |
| 1912 | First Balkan War, Turkey defeated. |
| 1913 | Second Balkan War, Bulgaria defeated. |
| 1914 | Assassination at Sarajevo, Austria declares war on Serbia, Russia orders a general mobilization, Germany declares war on Russia, France and invades Belgium. Britain declares war on Germany. |

## Guide to Questions

International relations 1871–1914 and the causes of the World War I cannot be understood without a sound knowledge of the historical geography of the period. Revise the maps on pages 61 and 64, then try this map question.

### Specimen Question 1

The Balkans 1908–14. Use the map opposite to answer the questions below.

*(Use place-names in your answer)*

a) *Name province A. Explain the international crisis surrounding it in 1908* (4)

b) *Write a brief account of the wars in the Balkans in 1912–13. Identify states D, E and F and comment on their respective attitudes at the conclusion of the conflict.* (8)

c) *Name state C. When was it created and for what reasons?* (3)

d) *Describe the events of 1914 in town B and trace their immediate consequences.* (5)

(Oxford and Cambridge, 1979)

When you have done it, check your answers with those on page 109.

**Specimen Question 2**

You need also to have a sound knowledge of the when?, who? and whys? of the main alliances, e.g.

*Why were the following agreements signed:*
a)  *The Dreikaiserbund 1881*
b)  *The Triple Alliance 1882*
c)  *The Dual Alliance 1893*
d)  *The Entente Cordiale 1904?*
(Cambridge, 1978)

This is a 'why' question and a tightly structured four-part one. Make sure that your answer is full of 'becauses' and its four main paragraphs linked precisely to (a), (b), (c) and (d). Check your dates since you could easily get (c) completely wrong.

**Suggested essay plan**   Four main paragraphs:

*1  Why the Dreikaiserbund?*   In 1881, this was a renewal of the original League of the Three Emperors of 1872. The Emperors were of Germany, Austro-Hungary and

Russia. Originally formed in 1873 because of a common desire to co-operate together against socialist revolution and to maintain international stability. In 1881 Bismarck was ready to renew it because his main aim was to prevent Russia and France joining a common alliance. Russia was ready to renew it because she felt isolated by the Dual Alliance of Germany and Austria (1879) and still distrusted democratic republican France. And Austria was ready to renew it because she hoped that it would curb Russia's ambitions in the Balkans, which ran counter to Austria's.

2 **Why the Triple Alliance 1882?**  This was signed by Germany and Austria, already allies by the Dual Alliance of 1879 and by Italy. Bismarck was its architect. He wanted it to increase the diplomatic isolation of France. Italy was keen to sign because she had ambitions in North Africa and feared that France, who had seized Tunisia the year before, might be planning to extend these conquests. Austria signed because, in the event of the collapse of the Turkish Empire in Europe, Italian support in the Balkans and Eastern Mediterranean could be useful.

3 **Why the Dual Alliance 1893?**  (Be careful here. This is not the Dual Alliance of 1879 referred to above but its later rival between France and Russia in 1893 from which the Triple Entente later developed.) France was keen to have this alliance because of the diplomatic isolation which Bismarck had created for her and because she faced colonial conflict with Britain. Russia signed because her previous alliances with Germany, the *Dreikaiserbund* and the Reinsurance Treaty, were out of date and hampered, rather than helped, her Balkan ambitions against Austria.

4 **Why the Entente Cordiale, 1904?**  This was an agreement between France and Britain on colonial matters, which provided the basis for future common action against Germany. Britain wanted it because she wished to come out of her previous 'splendid isolation'. She no longer had the economic and naval domination of the middle of the century. Colonial problems, like Fashoda and the Boer War, had caused much hostility in Europe. She felt particularly threatened by Germany, whose criticisms on colonial matters had been most harsh and whose new navy seemed to threaten Britain's basic security. For her part France needed all the friends she could get against Germany especially since, in 1904, her main ally, Russia, seemed more interested in the Far East than in Europe.

# Chapter 9 *Russia 1900–53*

Since the beginning of the twentieth century, the volcano of revolution had been murmuring close to the surface of Russian society. World War I created the conditions which caused it to erupt.

## The First Revolution

Badly led and armed the Russian armies were no match for the Germans. They suffered defeat after defeat and millions of casualties. In 1915 Tsar Nicholas II moved to the front to act as Commander-in-Chief. He was no help to his generals and left the government in the charge of his headstrong and foolish wife **Alexandra** and her extraordinary adviser, **Rasputin**—'the Mad Monk'. He was a drunken rogue completely unfit for any political responsibility. Guided by him and the Tsarina, the Russian government drifted out of touch with the realities of Russia's desperate situation. In 1916 a group of nobles assassinated Rasputin, but they were too late to save the Tsar's government. **Defeats** in battle continued. There was **economic chaos** and shortages of essential goods, including bread. In the major cities there were strikes and bread riots. Finally, in March (February according Russia's Julian calendar) 1917, troops in Petrograd refused to break up a strikers' demonstration. The Duma called on the Tsar to resign and set up a **Provisional Government** headed by Prince Lvov, a moderate reformer. Tsar Nicholas II abdicated without a struggle. So occurred the **first revolution** of 1917.

### The Provisional Government

The most dynamic member of the Provisional Government was **Kerensky**. Starting as Minister of Justice, he took over the direction of the war, and in July 1917, became Prime Minister. He and his colleagues made the fatal error of trying to **continue the war** with Germany and of **postponing major reforms** until the war was over. The war was unwinnable. Further defeats caused more casualties and spread demoralization, not only among the troops, but among the population generally. The economic situation remained grave. Public opinion turned against the Provisional Government and there were plenty of political opponents ready to take advantage of the changing mood.

### Russian Communist Party

One of the smallest opposing political parties was the most dangerous, the **Bolsheviks**. The word *bolshevik* means majority and they were the majority of the Russian Social Democratic or Communist Party when it had split in 1903. The Russian Communist Party had been founded by Plekhanov and was committed to the ideas of Marx and Engels.

The most important **Marxist ideas** are as follows. History is about the struggle between the social classes. Before the French Revolution of 1789 economic and therefore political power was held by kings and the noble (or upper) class. In

France in 1789, the **middle classes (bourgeoisie)** had overthrown the nobility and had developed the modern industrial state, through which they held economic control. The basic economic organization was 'capitalist'. Banks, factories, mines, indeed all important means of production, were owned, either directly or indirectly, through shares bought and sold on the stock market by middle-class men of property. The **workers (proletariat)** had no share in the ownership of their place of work and since the higher their wages the lower the profits of the owners, they were, so Marx and Engels argued, inevitably in a state of conflict with the bourgeoisie. The only solution was violent revolution. This would lead to a temporary dictatorship of the proletariat, from which a genuinely communist society would develop. All means of production would be publicly rather than privately owned and used for the common rather than individual need. A new era of brotherhood and co-operation would dawn.

The aim of the Russian Communist Party was to speed the coming of Communism to Russia. They split in 1903 over tactics. The Bolsheviks, led by **Lenin**, argued in favour of remaining a small group of totally committed revolutionaries, while the Mensheviks, the minority, led by **Martov** wanted to broaden the membership to include all those in favour of their main ideas.

# Lenin

Lenin had been born Vladimir Ulyanov in 1870. His father was a director of schools whose sons had a good education. Tragedy struck the family in 1886 when Alexander, the eldest son, was arrested and executed for plotting to assassinate the Tsar. From his university days Lenin was involved in revolutionary politics. Plekhanov introduced him to Marxism. Such was Lenin's **intelligence** that he developed Marxist ideas in relation both to the peasantry and to the spread of European power overseas. Such was his **grasp of practical politics** that by 1903 his leadership of the Bolsheviks was undisputed. Harassment from the secret police was continuous and he had to spend many years in exile, sometimes in Siberia, sometimes in Western Europe.

### The Second Revolution 1917
When the Tsar was overthrown, Lenin was in Switzerland. Judging correctly that this troublemaker might lessen the power of the Provisional Government to continue the war against them, the Germans transported him by train back to Russia. Lenin immediately stopped the Bolsheviks from co-operating in any way with the Provisional Government. He persuaded them that the time had come to prepare to seize power themselves. Their first attempt failed but, after **Kerensky's authority had been badly shaken** by the attempt of **General Kornilov** to overthrow him, they got ready to try again. Events were now moving in their favour. Kerensky was still trying to continue the war against Germany, yet soldiers were walking away from the front. Food and fuel were in short supply and winter was closing in. The Bolsheviks skilfully **increased their popularity**. 'End the War,' 'Land to the Peasants' and 'All Power to the *Soviets*' (workers' councils) were their slogans. They also built up their **support among key groups**, army and naval units, the soviets and factories. Finally in November (October by the Russian calendar)

Lenin felt strong enough to act. In ten days of street fighting Petrograd and Moscow were taken over. The opposition was dealt with ruthlessly. Kerensky was driven into exile. The recently elected Constituent Assembly dissolved, all other parties banned, censorship enforced and a secret police established.

## The Communists Survive 1918–22

The Bolsheviks believed that ruthlessness was essential if they were to survive. Certainly they were threatened from all directions. Seeing their danger more clearly than anyone, Lenin insisted that peace be made with Germany, despite the humiliating peace terms which Germany required in the *Treaty of Brest–Litovsk* (1918). He needed as many troops as he could get to fight off the attacks of the White (anti-communist) Russians who were backed by Britain, France, Japan and the USA. The *Civil War* lasted from 1918 to 1921 and to begin with a White victory seemed likely. However disputes amongst the White leaders, whose forces were scattered across thousands of miles, helped the Bolsheviks and the inspiring leadership of *Trotsky* transformed the *Red Army* from an indisciplined rabble into a tough and keen fighting force. By 1920 the Reds had the upper hand. They then had to fight a bitter frontier war with Poland, a nation which had been brought back into existence by the Versailles Settlement of 1919. Peace and the Russian/Polish frontier was eventually agreed by the *Treaty of Riga* 1921 and Russia had at last a kind of peace.

Yet that same year (1921) came another most dangerous crisis. During the Civil War, the Bolsheviks had imposed 'War Communism'. All major industries had been nationalized, agricultural production had been strictly supervised and tough measures taken against critics of government policy, even from within the Communist Party. Both in the cities and in the countryside opposition to these measures was growing. The sailors of the *Kronstadt* naval base had been among the Bolsheviks' most loyal supporters. In 1921 they mutinied, demanded new elections to the Soviets and arrested local Bolshevik officials. Trotsky had the mutiny put down by loyal army units but Lenin realized that the time had come to compromise. After much argument, he persuaded his comrades to agree to the *New Economic Policy* (NEP). It allowed considerably more private trading in market towns and rural areas and, though a clear step back from the basic Communist principle of public ownership, had the desired effect of increasing food production and the popularity of the government. This important and timely compromise is a good indication of Lenin's strength as a leader.

### A New State

In 1922, the Union of Soviet Socialist Republics (USSR) came into existence. It was built on two main foundations. The first was the *Soviets*, a pyramid of elected councils rising from local soviets to the National Congress of Soviets. The second was the *Communist Party*, the only political party allowed, with a select membership. It too was organized on a pyramid of committees with the Politburo as the chief political decision-maker.

### Lenin's Contribution

By now Lenin's health was failing and he died in 1924. Since this Bolshevik Revolution which he led has changed the history not just of Russia but the world, he is one of the outstanding figures in modern history. He was an unusual mixture of *political thinker* and *practical politician*. While his communist ideas offered an attractive vision of the future to the poor and underprivileged, the Bolshevik success in 1917 and their survival in the desperate years that followed was due to a large extent to his practical skills as a leader day by day. His special strengths were his determination, his clear grasp of priorities and sense of timing. He dominated his colleagues by his dedication and powers of argument. He was never a dictator, only the most influential member of the various top committees. He was also a genuinely humble man. He lived in a small apartment in the Kremlin with one old housekeeper to look after his rooms and do his mending. Nonetheless he was completely ruthless against those whom he considered to be the enemies of the revolution and allowed the secret police (CHEKA) to become a crucial part of the new Communist State.

## After Lenin

### The Struggle for Power
There were two main rivals for Lenin's position, Trotsky and Stalin. **Trotsky** was the favourite. He was brilliant and his services to the Revolution had been outstanding. Moreover Lenin had warned his leading comrades against Stalin on the grounds that he was rude and liable to abuse his power. It was **Stalin** however who by 1928 emerged as dictator of Russia and drove Trotsky into permanent exile.

Stalin was born Josef Dzhugashvili in 1879. His father was a poor shoemaker, his mother religious and ambitious for her son. He began training as a priest but was expelled for reading forbidden books. He became a Marxist and was in constant trouble with the police because of his revolutionary actions. He only played a small part in the October Revolution but steadily increased his influence in the Party by his organizing ability. Appointed Minister of Nationalities in 1918, he was promoted to the vital post of General Secretary of the Communist Party in 1922. As General Secretary he controlled appointments and promotions and he skilfully used this power to deal with Trotsky and other members of the Politburo. Unlike Lenin, he enjoyed personal power for its own sake. He was unhealthily suspicious of his colleagues and utterly without scruple and remorse in eliminating them.

An important principle as well as a clash of personalities underlay the dispute between Trotsky and Stalin in 1924. Trotsky was sure that an **international** communist revolution was possible and that Russia should take action to cause such a revolution. Stalin in contrast believed that Russia should first concentrate on building up her strength. Then and only then would she be able to give effective support to communists in other countries. '**Socialism in one country**' was his slogan and he was able to turn the Politburo against Trotsky on this issue.

### Stalin in power
Once firmly in control, Stalin set about making 'socialism in one country' a reality. The **expansion of heavy industry** was given top priority. His method was the Five-Year Plan. Ambitious targets were set for the expansion of key industries like coal, steel or tractor production. These targets had to be reached within a five-year period. The first Five-Year Plan ran from 1928 to 1932, the second from 1933 to 1937. Stalin's official statistics greatly exaggerated the success of the plans. Nonetheless there can be little doubt that they were a considerable achievement.

Non-communist economists estimate that Russia enjoyed an annual industrial growth rate of 17 per cent or more, a remarkable record especially in comparison with the dismal performance of the rest of the European economy during the depression years. There was a continuous shift of workers from farming into industry and large new towns were built in hitherto empty areas, like Magnitostroi in the Urals and Kuznetsstroi in Siberia. By 1939 the USSR had been transformed into a major industrial state. Otherwise she would not have been able to outfight the Germans between 1941 and 1945.

Another of Stalin's priorities was to **collectivize agriculture**. There was a serious food crisis in 1927, partly because the peasantry, using the freedom allowed them by the New Economic Policy, were hoarding grain so as to get better prices. Stalin insisted therefore that all peasants should join collective farms which should be owned by the state. In this way food production and distribution would be controlled, and more efficient farming methods developed. This collectivization policy was desperately resisted especially by the *kulaks*, the better-off peasants of the Ukraine. Many of them burnt their farms and slaughtered their livestock rather than submit. Stalin was unmoved. Peasants were killed or imprisoned in their millions and untold damage done to rural areas. Only in 1938 did agricultural output recover to 1928 levels. Nonetheless Russian farming was collectivized.

The experience of dictatorial power magnified Stalin's suspiciousness to mad lengths. In 1934 the murder of a leading Communist, Kirov, caused him to launch the first of a number of extraordinary **purges** against former Bolshevik colleagues. They were imprisoned and in much publicized 'show' trials forced to confess their 'plotting' against the Soviet people. Between 1937 and 1939 it was the turn of senior army officers. Hundreds were imprisoned or shot. Nor did the top levels of the secret police escape. Into the gaps made by his purges, Stalin promoted thousands of his yes-men. His own position was stronger than ever.

1941–8 were his best years. Though taken by surprise by the German invasion of 1941, he gave Russia courageous, steadfast and intelligent leadership both in the black years of defeat 1941–2 and the later years of victory. In the Great-Power diplomacy at the end of the War he had strong cards and played them well to win Russia a **dominating position** in Europe and the world. (See page 97).

These successes did nothing to mellow his final years. His suspiciousness remained. Millions of possible opponents were held in prison or in labour camps. Thousands of returning prisoners of war were also placed in these camps for many years, because Stalin feared that their contact with other countries might have infected them with unacceptable ideas. Priority was still given to strengthening heavy industry and the armed forces. Stalin showed no interest in making life more comfortable or interesting for the Russian people. He lived an isolated unreal life surrounded by flatterers who were terrified of him. Just as he was considering another purge in 1953 he died.

Stalin is a most controversial figure. His achievements were great. By his single-minded insistence on rapid industrialization he supervised the development of an economic strength which made possible the defeat of Germany in the 1940s and super-power policies in the 1950s. He won for Russia a position in Europe and the world far stronger than any previous ruler in her history. But the price he exacted for these achievements was horrific. He caused more Russian deaths than Hitler! He made terror a fact of Russian political life. He all but destroyed intellectual, literary, artistic and musical creativity. And the road along which he drove Russian Communism would have been neither recognized nor respected by Marx and Lenin.

## The Main Events

| | |
|---|---|
| 1914 | World War I begins, power of Tsarina and Rasputin grows. |
| 1916 | Rasputin murdered by nobles. |
| 1917 Feb/March | (The First Revolution) Duma forces abdication of Tsar Nicholas, Provisional Government set up under Prince Lvov. Kerensky a leading member. |
| April | Lenin returns from Switzerland. |
| Summer | Kornilov Conspiracy. |
| Oct/Nov | Successful Bolshevik Revolution (the Second Revolution). |
| 1918 | Treaty of Brest–Litovsk with Germany. |
| 1918–21 | Civil War. |
| 1920–1 | War with Poland, ended by the Treaty of Riga. |
| 1921 | Kronstadt Mutiny, New Economic Policy. |
| 1924 | Death of Lenin. |
| 1924–8 | Struggle for power between Stalin and Trotsky. |
| 1928–53 | Stalin effectively dictator of Russia. |
| 1928 | First Five-Year Plan. |
| 1929 | Trotsky driven into exile. |
| | Forced collectivization of agriculture begins. |
| 1933 | Second Five-Year Plan. |
| 1935–9 | Period of Purges. |
| 1939 | Nazi-Soviet Pact. |
| 1941 | Germans invade Russia. |
| 1945 | War War II ends. |
| 1945–8 | Soviet take-over of Eastern Europe. |
| 1953 | Death of Stalin. |

## Some Important Terms

| | |
|---|---|
| Communists | followers of the ideas of Marx and Engels. |
| Bolsheviks | the majority of the Russian Communist Party who followed Lenin when the Party split in 1903. |
| Mensheviks | the minority of the Russian Communist Party who opposed Lenin during and after the 1903 split. |
| Soviets | workers' councils, set up during the 1905 and 1917 revolutions. |
| Duma | the parliamentary assembly set up after the 1905 Revolution. |
| Politburo | the most powerful committee of the Russian Communist Party after 1917. |

| | |
|---|---|
| *Kulaks* | the better-off peasantry of the Ukraine. |
| Reds | Communist supporters. |
| Whites | anti-Communists. |

## Guide to Questions

You should concentrate on three main themes: the causes and events of the 1917 Revolutions (see Further Questions page 103); Lenin; and Stalin.

### Specimen Question 1

*What part was played by Lenin in the establishment of the USSR?* (Oxford, 1979)

Since Lenin played the leading part in the creation of the USSR, you are in fact being asked to describe Lenin's achievements from 1917 to 1924 in so far as they led to the Union of Soviet Socialist Republics replacing the Imperial Russian Empire. You will have plenty of information at your fingertips. Concentrate on setting it out clearly and logically and jot down some paragraph headings in rough before you start.

**Suggested essay plan**   I would have five main paragraph headings:

*1  Lenin as Bolshevik leader to 1917*   Intelligent (develops Marx's ideas), dedicated, leads the Bolsheviks through the split of 1903 and holds them together in exile.

*2  Lenin and the Revolutions of 1917*   Once back in Russia, thanks to the Germans, leads Bolsheviks into continuous opposition to Provisional Government; clear about the right policies to win support, organizes seizure of power at exactly the right moment; absolutely ruthless with opposition, e.g. Constituent Assembly disbanded, opposition parties banned, secret police, Tsar and family murdered.

*3  Lenin and the Years of War 1918–21*   'Will the Bolsheviks survive?' is the main question of these years; an important step towards survival is Lenin's insistence that peace is secured with Germany at any price (Treaty of Brest-Litovsk 1918) then leads government at home while Trotsky leads war effort against Poles and Whites.

*4  Lenin and the New Economic Policy 1921–4*   NEP another vital measure if Bolsheviks to stay in power, Kronstadt Mutiny 1921 persuades Lenin that a compromise with Communist economic principles essential; allows some return of private enterprise in countryside and smaller towns.

*5  Lenin and the government structure of Russia*   Not a dictator, a leading member of governing committees, these committees organize government on two main foundations, the Soviets from local Soviets to the National Congress of Soviets and the Communist Party, the only political party allowed, which was headed by the Politburo. The Union of Soviet Socialist Republics officially came into existence in December 1922. By that date, Lenin's health was failing and he died in 1924. Plainly his part in the establishment of the USSR was the leading one.

### Specimen Question 2

*Study the cartoon of the late 1930s on page 76, and then answer questions (a) to (e) which follow:*

*a)  Identify (i) the country partly shown and partly named on the map beside the desk, and (ii) the someone of whom Josef seems to remind the standing man. (2)*

"IT'S QUEER HOW YOU REMIND ME OF SOMEONE, JOSEF . . ."
Stalin

b) *Explain the significance of the name on the book held by the standing man, and show why this contributed to his puzzlement.* (4)

c) *To what recent Russian developments did the letter-trays on the desk refer?* (4)

d) *(i) What international agreements in 1939 united the two men shown in the cartoon in photographs (one on the wall and one on the desk)?*
*(ii) In what circumstances was this agreement shattered?* (4)

e) *How appropriate, in your opinion, was the cartoonist's implied comparison between the two key figures in the cartoon?* (6)

(*Evidence in Question,* Watson, Rayner and Stapley)

Complete it on your own. Then check your answers against those on page 110.

# Chapter 10 *The Versailles Settlement and the League of Nations*

When, after months of argument at Versailles near Paris, final agreement of the peace settlement was reached in 1919, the young and brilliant economist J. K. Keynes resigned from the British delegation. He wrote to Lloyd George, Britain's Prime Minister as follows: 'I am slipping away from this scene of nightmare. I can do no more good here. I've gone on hoping even through these last dreadful weeks that you'd find some way of making the Treaty a just document. But now it is apparently too late.' Soon afterwards Keynes published a fierce criticism of the Versailles Settlement called *The Economic Consequences of the Peace*. The Settlement has remained controversial ever since.

The task facing the peacemakers was enormous, much greater than that which had faced the peacemakers at Vienna a hundred years earlier. World War I had been by far the most expensive war in human history, both in human casualties and in the destruction of property. Lasting much longer than expected, it had left both winners and losers exhausted and bitter. **Germany** had collapsed into revolution, **Russia**'s Communist revolutionary government was struggling to survive a civil war. The **Austrian Empire** had fragmented into a patchwork of new nations, so too had the **Turkish Empire** giving rise to numerous boundary disputes. Another question to be faced was what should happen to Germany's overseas empire.

## The Fourteen Points

Once it became clear to the German leaders in the late summer of 1918 that the war was lost, they asked for a negotiated peace on the basis of the Fourteen Points which President Wilson of the USA had put forward the previous January. These were as follows:

1) Peace treaties should be open, not secret.
2) The oceans of the world should be free to navigation in peace and war.
3) There should be no economic barriers between nations.
4) Armaments should be kept to the lowest possible level.
5) The interests of the colonial populations should be considered when the future of colonies were decided.
6) All Russian territory should be evacuated.
7) Belgium should be evacuated and her lands restored.
8) French lands should be evacuated and Alsace–Lorraine restored.
9) The principle of nationality should more clearly determine Italy's boundaries.
10) The peoples of the Austrian Empire should have the chance to determine their futures.
11) The lands of Romania, Serbia and Montenegro should be restored and Serbia to gain a coastline.
12) The Turkish parts of the Turkish (Ottoman) Empire should gain independence. The other peoples of this Empire should have a say in their future, and

the Dardanelles should become an international seaway.

13) An independent Poland, made up of land clearly Polish, with access to the sea, should be created.

14) A general association of nations should be established to maintain peace.

In the settlement of 1919, some of these points were honoured (7, 8, 12 and 14), some were partly honoured (5, 9 and 13) some were ignored (1, 2, 3 and 4) and the rest decided by events outside the control of the men at Versailles. Other decisions were made which were not included in the original Fourteen Points. The Germans complained that the Final Settlement was far harsher than the Fourteen Points on which they had agreed to negotiate.

## The Peacemakers

The negotiations at Versailles were dominated by the **Big Three**, Wilson for the USA, Clemenceau for France and Lloyd George for Britain. They were very different personalities. **Wilson** knew that he represented the most powerful nation in the world and came to Europe with a vision of a new and better world which could be created out of the shambles of war. He received a most enthusiastic reception from ordinary Europeans and was convinced that they shared his idealism. He was determined to achieve a fair and moderate peace which would be preserved by his brainchild, the **League of Nations**. Thus World War I would prove to be the war that ended wars. **Clemenceau** of France was a contrast, old, tough and cynical. In his lifetime, France had twice been invaded by the Germans. His only real interest was the security of France which should be achieved by a harsh peace which would keep Germany weak for many years to come. **Lloyd George** for Britain was an experienced and cunning politician but he was in a difficult position. Though he was personally in favour of a moderate settlement, British public opinion wanted the hated and defeated enemy to be crushed. Consequently the final settlement was a harsh one.

It consisted of five separate treaties. The main one, of Versailles, (1919) was with Germany, of St Germain (1920) with Austria, of Trianon (1920) with Hungary, of Neuilly (1919) with Bulgaria, and of Sèvres (1920) with Turkey. The Sèvres Treaty did not work and was replaced in 1923 by the Treaty of Lausanne.

## The Terms of the Settlement

### Territorial Changes

**Germany lost** Posen, the Polish Corridor and part of Upper Silesia to Poland; Danzig became a free city; another section of Upper Silesia went to the new nation of Czechoslovakia. In addition, Eupen and Malmédy went to Belgium. North Schleswig to Denmark. Alsace and Lorraine to France, while the Saar was to be administered by the League of Nations. A broad area on both sides of the Rhine, known as the demilitarized zone, was forbidden to German troops.

**The Austrian Empire disappeared.** Austria changed into a small nation with 6,500,000 inhabitants. The former provinces of Bosnia, Herzegovina, Croatia and Slovenia joined Serbia and Montenegro to form a new, mainly South Slav nation, **Yugoslavia**. A large section of Hungary went to Romania, what was left became

The Versailles Settlement (of Europe)

independent. The Czechs and Slovaks came together as independent Czechoslovakia, Galicia went to Poland and Istria, South Tyrol and Trentino to Italy. Fiume was the cause of a long dispute between Italy and Yugoslavia. Eventually (1924) Yugoslavia got most of it.

*Poland reappeared* on the map of Europe after an absence of more than a century. The eastern border was finally agreed by the Treaty of Riga (1921) which ended a war between the Poles and Communist Russia. Lithuania, Latvia, Estonia and Finland, former Russian provinces, became independent. Bulgaria suffered small losses to Yugoslavia and to Greece.

*Greece made considerable gains from Turkey* by the Treaty of Sèvres, including Smyrna on the eastern shores of the Aegean. However, the humiliating Sèvres terms helped to cause a revolution in Turkey. Kemal, who is often known as Kemal Ataturk, overthrew the Sultan and defeated the Greeks at Smyrna even though they had the support of the British, French and Italians. By the Treaty of Lausanne, Kemal won back most of the land lost to Turkey by the Treaty of Sèvres.

Outside Europe, the former *Turkish and German possessions* were distributed among the victors. Point 5 of the Fourteen Points, that consideration be given to the interests of the colonial peoples was to some extend safe-guarded by the 'mandate' system whereby the governing power was supervised by the League of Nations and required to prepare the colony for eventual independence. To Britain went the mandates for Palestine, Iraq, Transjordan and Tanganyika; to France, Syria and the Cameroons; to Belgium Ruanda–Urundi and to South Africa German South-West Africa. German possessions in the Far East were divided up similarly.

**Self-Determination** was the principle of President Wilson which underlay Points 9, 10 and 11 of the Fourteen Points that wherever possible, and especially in Central and Eastern Europe, peoples with a common sense of nationhood, which stemmed from a common language, culture and history, should govern themselves. For the most part this was achieved in Europe and the new frontiers generally followed boundaries between nationalities. However there were some important exceptions. For example, the new Poland included a number of minority groups, the most important being German. For geographical and defensive reasons, the mainly German Sudetenland region was given to Czechoslovakia. In fact the one nationality to whom self-determination was not allowed was the German. Another clause of the Versailles Treaty forbade German-speaking Austria to unite with Germany. Hitler and the Nazis were able to make much of this apparent unfairness in the 1930s.

### Reparations
These were the damages which Germany was forced to pay to help the victors repair the destruction caused by World War I. They were eventually fixed at £6,600,000,000 in 1921. Germany also had to hand over all merchant ships over 1,600 tons, and to give coal, horses, sheep and cattle to France, Belgium and Italy. Military forces: Germany could have only six battleships and no submarines. Her army could not rise above 100,000. Conscription was forbidden. So was an air force.

**War Guilt** According to Article 231 of the Versailles Treaty, Germany agreed that the war had been caused by the aggression of Germany and her allies. The aim of this clause was to justify the demand for reparations. The Germans thought it most unfair.

### The Versailles Settlement: an Evaluation
Though the settlement was the work of able and determined men making the best of exceptionally difficult circumstances, their critics have been able to make out a

powerful case. J. M. Keynes' arguments are especially worth noting. His first criticism was that the settlement was *too harsh*. Lasting peace seldom follows if the defeated feel humiliated—which is how the Germans felt in 1919. Furthermore reparations could never make *economic sense*. Germany had been gravely weakened by an economic blockade during the war and was in no position to raise so huge a sum. In addition the settlement ignored the economic realities of Europe which had grown rich before the war by international trade. The attempt to keep Germany and Austria poor by demanding reparations would weaken their ability to take part in international trade and the whole continent, including the victors would suffer as well.

Later events proved Keynes correct for the most part. The Germans only signed the treaty in 1919 because they were threatened with war if they did not. They believed it to be extremely unfair and did their utmost to avoid paying reparations. One reason why Hitler and the Nazis grew so popular was their clear determination to defy the terms of the Versailles Treaty. The economic recovery of Europe in the 1920s was very slow and the payment of reparations a constant problem. They were never paid in full.

The territorial settlement also proved unsatisfactory, especially in Eastern Europe. The *German minorities* never came to terms with being ruled by Poles or Czechs and the new *small nations* of Eastern Europe were caught between two major powers, Germany and Russia. In 1919, both these countries were temporarily weak but, once they had recovered, they were a worrying threat to their smaller neighbours.

These weaknesses would have been less serious if the international peace-keeping organization, in which President Wilson had such great hopes, had worked. But this, the League of Nations, also had *serious shortcomings*. From the start it failed to include Germany or Russia and, sadly and surprisingly, the USA. During his long stay in Europe Wilson lost touch with American public opinion and failed to realize how irritated it was becoming with quarrelsome Europeans. The American Congress refused to agree to America joining. This was a terrible setback—and not only for the League. France had only agreed to sign the treaties because they seemed to be guaranteed by the USA acting through the League of Nations.

## The League of Nations 1919–39

This organization nonetheless played an important part in international events between the two world wars.

Its headquarters were in Geneva. Its Council met regularly three times a year and consisted of four Permanent Members (Britain, France, Italy and Japan) and four Non-Permanent ones. The Council was *intended to be able to take prompt action* when necessary and there was also an annual Assembly in which all member nations were represented. On major policies, Council and Assembly had to be unanimous and each member state could use its veto to prevent the League taking action. The chief official was the Secretary-General, the first being a Briton, Sir Eric Drummond. There was also the International Court of Justice with its headquarters at the Hague in the Netherlands, the International Labour Organization, and a number of special commissions supervising internationally sensitive problems like the mandates, refugees and minorities. Some of the most effective work of the League was done by the special commissions.

In international crises, the League was **never very effective**. The power of **veto** frequently prevented it being decisive. The absence of Russia, Germany and the USA meant that only a strong lead from France and Britain could make it a powerful influence, but the support from these two Great Powers was seldom more than **lukewarm**.

Its best years were in the 1920s. It successfully made Danzig a free city, despite the rivalries of the Germans and Poles. It settled the Polish–German frontier dispute in Upper Silesia. In 1921 it ended a dispute between Sweden and Finland over the Aaland Islands, ruling in favour of Finland. In 1922 it saved Austria from economic collapse, in 1923 it limited, though it could not prevent, Italian aggression against Greece over Corfu, and in 1925 it halted a Greek invasion of Bulgaria. Much was done to end the refugee problem and to check the spread of epidemic diseases. However, there were failures too, e.g. the Poland versus Lithuania dispute over Vilna in 1920.

In the 1930s its failure was complete. In 1931 **its authority was challenged** by one of its leading members, **Japan**, who **invaded Chinese Manchuria**. The League voted in China's favour but Japan continued the invasion and left the League. Much now depended upon whether Britain and France were ready to lead the League in positive action against Japan. They were not and the Japanese were seen by the world to have got away with their aggression.

The European dictators, Hitler and Mussolini, took note of Japan's success. Germany had joined the League in 1926, but Hitler took her out when he became Chancellor and began rapid rearmament in open defiance of the Versailles Settlement, which the League was supposed to defend. Again Britain and France were unready to work through the League. On the contrary, Britain tried to negotiate her own agreements with Hitler. The worst blow, however, came from **Mussolini** whose army **invaded Abyssinia** in 1935. The Italian dictator boasted that his aim was conquest. The Abyssinian Emperor, Haile Selassie, eloquently appealed to the League for help. At last the League seemed ready to take firm action. Not only did it condemn Italy but agreed to enforce economic sanctions against her. However in 1935 and 1936, Britain and France were more frightened of Germany and wished to avoid pushing Mussolini into Hitler's arms. So they refused to allow the vital economic sanction, the cutting of oil supplies, to be used. Mussolini pressed on. Abyssinia was conquered and Haile Selassie's prediction that if the League failed to come to Abyssinia's aid then the world would soon be at war again proved true. Italy's successful defiance over Abyssinia was effectively the end of the League of Nations.

## The Main Events

| | |
|---|---|
| 1918 January | President Wilson announces his Fourteen Points. |
| November | World War I ends. |
| 1919 | Peace negotiations at Versailles. Treaty of Versailles with Germany. |
| | Treaty of Neuilly with Bulgaria. |

| 1920 | Treaty of St Germain with Austria, of Trianon with Hungary, of Sèvres with Turkey. League of Nations established in Geneva. |
| 1921 | Treaty of Riga ends Russian–Polish War. League settles Aaland Islands dispute between Sweden and Finland. |
| 1922 | League provides economic aid to Austria. |
| 1925 | League halts Greek invasion of Bulgaria. |
| 1926 | Germany joins the League. |
| 1931 | Japan invades Manchuria. |
| 1933 | Japan leaves the League over Manchuria. Germany leaves the League to rearm. |
| 1935–6 | Mussolini invades Abyssinia and successfully defies the League. |
| 1936–9 | German, Italian and Japanese aggression increases. |
| 1939 | World War II begins. |

## Some Important Terms

| Minorities | racial groups smaller in number and different from the racial majority in a particular country, e.g. Germans in Poland. |
| Self-determination | the principle that a people conscious of their common nationhood should have the right to independence. |
| Mandate | the administration by European countries of overseas territories under the supervision of the League of Nations. |
| Veto | the power to prevent action being taken. Veto is the Latin for 'I forbid'. |
| Reparations | the money from Germany and her allies to pay for the destruction of World War I. |

## Guide to Questions

Not surprisingly, map questions on the Versailles Settlement are popular. A typical one can be found as one of the further questions to consider on page 103. Make sure that you have revised the map on page 79 before trying it. Evidence questions also appear, e.g.

### Specimen Question 1

*Study this extract from Lloyd George's statement of British War Aims in January, 1918, and then answer questions (a) to (g) which follow.*

*The first requirement always put forward by the British Government and their Allies has been the complete restoration, political, territorial and economic, of the independence of Belgium and such reparation as can be made for the devastation of its towns and provinces.*

*Next comes the restoration of Serbia, Montenegro and the occupied parts of*

*France, Italy and Romania. The complete withdrawal of the alien armies and the reparation for injustice done is a fundamental condition of permanent peace.*

*We mean to stand by French democracy to the death in the demand they make for a reconsideration of the great wrong in 1871 when, without any regard to the wishes of the population, two French provinces were torn from the side of France and incorporated in the German Empire.*

*We believe that an independent Poland, comprising all those genuinely Polish elements who desire to form part of it, is an urgent necessity for the stability of Western Europe.*

*Similarly, though we agree with President Wilson that the break-up of Austria–Hungary is not part of our war aims, we feel that, unless genuine self-government on true democratic principles is granted to those Austro–Hungarian nationalities who have long desired it, it is impossible to hope for the removal of those causes of unrest in that part of Europe which have so long threatened its general peace.*

(*War Memoirs*, Lloyd George, Nicholson and Watson.)

a) *President Wilson made a similar statement of his war aims. By what title were Wilson's war aims known?* (1)
b) *Suggest the reason why Lloyd George* first *made reference to Belgium.* (2)
c) *Why did Lloyd George speak of the need to restore Serbia? What provision was made for Serbia in the peace settlement of 1919–20?* (1 + 2)
d) *Name the two provinces lost by France in 1871 and state what provision was made for them in the Treaty of Versailles.* (2)
e) *In what sense did Lloyd George use the term* reparation? *In what ways were the defeated powers, after 1918, required to make* reparation? (4)
f) *Describe the decisions made in the peace settlement of 1919–20 in relation to Poland and account for the fact that they were resented by many Germans.* (4)
g) *Explain briefly how the principles laid down by Lloyd George in relation to Austria–Hungary were implemented in the peace settlement of 1919–20.* (4)

(London, 1976)

With every 'evidence' question remember to consider carefully what position the writer held, the date he was writing and his likely bias. This extract dates from 1918, when the war was still raging. As Britain's Prime Minister, Lloyd George is likely to be writing with his country's interests foremost in his mind. When you have written your answers, compare them with those on page 110.

Here are two typical multiple-choice questions, one on the treaties, the other on the League of Nations.

**Specimen Question 2**

*One of the objects of the League of Nations, referred to in the Covenant, was*
*A the abolition of collective security*
*B the collection of reparations*
*C the elimination of democracy*
*D the reduction of armaments*
*E the suppression of communism.*
(*New Objective Tests in Twentieth Century History*, Rayner, Stapley and Watson)

Always with multiple-choice questions, work your way to the correct answer by a process of elimination. It cannot be A since the League of Nations was created to achieve collective security. Nor can it be C since Wilson and leading members of the League, like France and Britain, were strongly democratic. It cannot be E since Wilson was not strongly anti-communist and Russia later joined. So it must either be B or D. In fact since the reduction of armaments was always an important Wilsonian ideal, while the collection of reparations was a particular problem not involving the League as a whole, the correct answer is D.

## Specimen Question 3

*Which of the following treaties was NOT imposed on one of the defeated Central Powers at the end of World War I? A Brest-Litovsk*

*B Neuilly*
*C St Germain*
*D Sèvres*
*E Versailles*

*(New Objective Tests in Twentieth Century History,* Rayner, Stapley and Watson)

Again work to the correct answer by elimination. It cannot be E, Versailles, because that was the treaty with Germany, nor D, Sèvres, because that was with Turkey, nor C, St Germain, because that was with Austria, nor B, Neuilly, since that was with Bulgaria. So it must be A, Brest–Litovsk, which was in fact the treaty imposed by Germany early in 1918 on the defeated Russians. It is worth remembering that all the treaties which ended World War I and made up the Versailles Settlement were signed in France at places not far from Paris.

# Chapter 11 *Germany and Nazism 1919–39*

Looking back at the early successes of the Nazi Party, Ludecke, himself a Nazi, gave this explanation: 'all over the land young spirits were rising up in defiant protest against the wretchedness of a life which their fathers seemed to have spoiled for them'.

## The Weimar Republic

The post-war years were wretched. From the first the new democratic republic struggled to survive. (It is usually described as the Weimar Republic because it first met in the peaceful country town of Weimar rather than strife-torn Berlin.) Its leaders had to sign the hated peace treaty and so gained great unpopularity. The Communist Party (KPD) wanted to overthrow it, so did many Nationalists who included among their number army officers. From 1918 to 1922 the country was in **confusion** with widespread rioting, attempts at revolution and assassinations. In 1923 the French occupied the important industrial region of the Ruhr, with the aim of forcing the reluctant Germans to pay **reparations** more promptly. The effect of the Ruhr occupation was **inflation** on a catastrophic scale which destroyed, within a few weeks, the value of the German currency and with it the savings of millions of families. That same year an extreme nationalist party, the NSDAP or Nazis, attempted but failed to seize power in Munich. The Nazi leader, **Adolf Hitler**, was given a short prison sentence.

While **Stresemann** was first Chancellor then Foreign Minister, from 1923 to 1929, there was an improvement both in economic conditions and in relations with other major European Powers. Then, in 1929, came the **Wall Street Crash**, which led to a great economic depression first in the USA and then in Europe. Germany, whose economic recovery after 1923 was based on American loans, was affected particularly badly. By 1932 more than six million Germans were unemployed and despair was widespread.

## Hitler and the Nazi Party

Within the Weimar Republic were a multitude of political parties, but the one which benefited most from this economic disaster was Hitler's Nazi Party. Before 1929 it was a small extreme nationalist and anti-semitic party with only 12 seats in the *Reichstag* (Parliament). By 1932 it had grown to the largest single party with 230 seats.

Hitler was born an Austrian. He had a poor school record and, in the years before World War I, lived in Vienna in desperate poverty trying to make a living as an artist. Already as a young man he was a **fervent German patriot** who wanted German-speaking Austria to be part of a greater Germany which would dominate

Europe. He greeted World War I with enthusiasm, joined the German army and fought bravely on the Western Front, eventually gaining modest promotion to corporal. Like millions of other German soldiers, he refused to believe that they had been defeated on the battlefield. Rather he was convinced that a conspiracy of Jews and Communists back in Berlin had stabbed the magnificent German army in the back. The Treaty of Versailles was an **unjust humiliation** on the German people which should be avenged as soon as they regained their strength. From the army he drifted into extreme politics and in 1923 tried and failed to seize power in Munich, the provincial capital of Bavaria. The nine months in prison, which followed this failure, he put to good use by writing *Mein Kampf* (*My Struggle*) which is partly an autobiography and partly a statement of his political views.

The most important of these were about race. Hitler was a **racialist**. He believed that the Aryan or German race was superior to all others and should naturally dominate Europe and the world. Among the inferior races, whose function was to serve the master-race, were the Slavs of Eastern Europe and Negroes. The Jews were a special case. They were evil as well as inferior and constantly plotting to prevent the master-race from achieving its rightful dominant position.

Another important belief, about **lebensraum** or living-space followed from his racialism. Since the Aryans did not have enough room to live as they should in Central Europe, they must expand into Eastern Europe at the expense of the inferior Slavs. That this might mean a major war did not trouble Hitler. He had nothing but contempt for the Versailles Settlement and for the League of Nations. He also had **contempt for democracy**. A greater Germany could only come if it were a single people united with a common purpose under a single leader (i.e. a one-party dictatorship of him and his Nazis.) For Communism he had both contempt and hatred, partly because it was the brainchild of a Jew, Karl Marx, and partly because it preferred international brotherhood to national glory.

To millions of anxious and bitter Germans between 1929 and 1930, these ideas appeared much more sensible than they do today. They were a proud people convinced that they deserved a dominating position in Europe. Anti-semitism was popular all over Europe. Democracy did seem to be failing and one-party dictatorships, e.g. Mussolini in Italy, to be working better. Russian Communism was generally feared. And by constantly criticizing the Versailles Settlement and by calling on all Germans to cease their conflicts and join together in common purpose he encouraged a unity which was felt to be the overriding national need.

### The Nazis' Rise to Power

The tactics of Hitler and his associates between 1929 and 1933 were skilful. They energetically toured the country **speech-making** and organizing **spectacular demonstrations**. Hitler was an outstanding public speaker and Goebbels a propagandist of genius. As unemployment grew worse law and order broke down in many German cities. The **private army** of the Nazis (the SA or Brownshirts) brawled in the streets with their main rivals the Communists and usually won. Simultaneously Hitler won over senior army officers by his criticisms of the Versailles Settlement; the businessmen and the middle classes by his anti-Communism and his determination to restore unity, law and order; and working people by offering hope for the future. In 1932 he felt strong enough to challenge Field Marshal von Hindenburg for the Presidency of the Republic. Though he lost, by 53 per cent of the votes to 37 per cent he was now clearly one of Germany's most powerful political personalities.

Political violence increased and weak coalition governments came and went.

In the elections of November 1932, Nazi strength in the *Reichstag* fell back from 230 seats to 196. This was one reason why, in January 1933, when yet another coalition government had failed, experienced politicians, led by von Papen, persuaded Hindenburg, the President, to invite Hitler to become Chancellor in another coalition. They would have no difficulty they argued with all their years of experience in keeping Hitler and his Nazis on a leash—the opposite happened.

## Hitler in Power

Using the power of the Chancellorship, Hitler broke loose and by the summer of 1933 had established a one-party dictatorship. This is how he did it. The first step was to insist that **new elections** be held. These were fixed for March 1933. At the end of February, the German people were horrified to learn that the *Reichstag* had been burnt down. The Nazis said that the Communists were to blame and arrested a Dutch half-wit with communist connections to prove their point. They then arrested most of the Communist leaders. Today most historians believe that the fire was probably the work of the Nazis themselves who then framed the Communists. In the March election the Nazis won 288 seats. This did not give them control on their own but they got the support of the right-wing National and Catholic Centre parties which allowed the passing of the **Enabling Acts**. The effect of these was to shift supreme political power from the *Reichstag* to the Chancellor personally. To all intents and purposes the Enabling Act made Hitler **dictator**.

The results were immediate and drastic. All political parties other than the Nazis were banned. Trades unions were abolished and strikes forbidden. Only two groups remained as possible rivals to Hitler. The first, **the German army**, was still outside the Nazi movement but the second, **the SA** headed by Röhm, was within. Röhm was an old friend of Hitler's but increasingly unhappy with his leader's friendliness with businessmen and army officers. Röhm was a genuine revolutionary who wanted a thorough shake-up of German society and a Nazi takeover of the army. Hitler dealt with both these rivals in 1934. The army generals promised him their total support if he would get rid of Röhm. On the so-called 'Night of the Long Knives' of April 1934, Hitler invited Röhm and other leaders of the SA to a party conference and there had them murdered. Soon afterwards President Hindenburg died and Hitler proclaimed himself *Führer* and Reich Chancellor. Every German soldier took a personal oath of loyalty to him, while 90 per cent of the German people voted by plebiscite in favour of his new position.

### Nazi Policy

In their methods of government the Nazis were '**totalitarian**'. They despised individual freedom and aimed to achieve the **total** control of the lives of their countrymen.

An important part of such totalitarianism was **censorship**. As Minister of Propaganda, Goebbels controlled the output of German radio, newspapers and films. Books of which the Nazis disapproved were burnt.

German youth was a major target of Nazis **propaganda**. Either teachers joined the Nazi Teachers League or they were sacked. Textbooks were re-written to fit the Nazi philosophy. Considerable pressure was put on children to join Nazi organizations like the Hitler Youth for boys and the League of German Maidens for the girls. The aim of these organizations was to produce citizens fit in body and Nazi in mind.

Hitler quickly began to make his **anti-semitism** a reality. From 1935 Jews could no longer become German citizens nor marry Aryans. Thousands lost their jobs and thousands, especially the best educated, emigrated. Those millions who stayed suffered increasing persecution as the years passed. Attacks on property were followed by personal violence and eventually the concentration camps and the mass murders of the 'Final Solution'.

After an unsuccessful attempt to create a Reich Church which was both Christian and Nazi, German church leaders were persecuted. By 1937 thousands of priests were imprisoned in concentration camps.

Nonetheless Hitler was very popular with the majority of Germans. This was mainly because in economic and foreign affairs, his government proved **successful**. Economic recovery was swift and remarkable. A much publicized 'Battle for Work' created many temporary jobs while rearmament and new public works meant more permanent employment. Simultaneously there was a world-wide economic recovery. Hitler was well served by his clever Minister of Finance, Dr Schacht. **Unemployment fell** from six million in 1932 to less than a million four years later. In the same period Germany's national income doubled.

**Foreign Policy**

This was Hitler's main interest. He was determined to destroy the Versailles Settlement and to dominate Europe peacefully where possible but by war if necessary. The main defence of the Versailles Settlement were the League of Nations and the two 'Great Power' members of the League, Britain and France. By 1933, the **League was faltering**. The **Japanese** had openly and successfully defied its rulings over Manchuria and **Mussolini** was soon to do the same over Abyssinia. Within Britain there was a strong body of opinion that the Versailles Settlement was unfair to Germany and certainly not worth a major war. In contrast the French believed it to be essential to their safety. Between 1920 and 1923 they had formed a defensive alliance, often known as the 'Little Entente' of Romania, Czechoslovakia, Yugoslavia and themselves to maintain the Settlement against a reviving Germany. However in the 1930s France was divided by bitter internal divisions and never felt strong enough to act against Germany without the support of Britain. From 1933 to 1939 **Hitler was able to play upon these weaknesses**. His successes were continuous and spectacular.

**Rearmament**   In 1933, he took Germany out of the League of Nations. In 1934, he began a massive rearmament programme in direct breach of the Versailles Treaty. The following year, skilfully using Britain's impatience with France who was trying to insist that the Versailles Settlement be firmly maintained, he persuaded Britain to sign a **joint naval agreement**, again a breach of the Versailles Treaty.

**The Rhineland 1936**   He ordered the German army to re-occupy the zone demilitarized by the Versailles Treaty. This was his boldest step yet, since the movement of troops could be seen as a direct threat to the French. Indeed the French were ready to take military action but the British refused to back them. Hitler had gambled and won. He was convinced that in a crisis Britain and France were gutless and it would be worth gambling for higher stakes.

**The Axis and anti-Comintern Pact 1936 and the Spanish Civil War 1936–9**   The Rome–Berlin Axis was the agreement of Mussolini and Hitler to follow a common

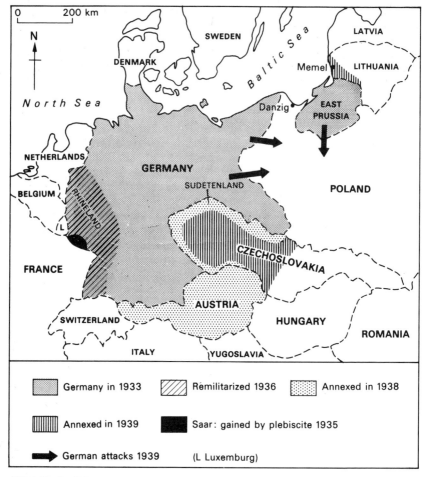

Map legend:

- Germany in 1933
- Remilitarized 1936
- Annexed in 1938
- Annexed in 1939
- Saar: gained by plebiscite 1935
- German attacks 1939    (L Luxemburg)

Hitler's Foreign Policy

foreign policy. It was most effective in Spain, where German bombers and Italian troops played a considerable part in helping General Franco to victory over the Republicans, who had some support from Communist Russia and European socialist parties. In the same year he persuaded Japan to agree to the anti-Comintern Pact, an anti-communist alliance directed against Russia.

**Austria and the Anschluss 1938**   Within Austria a lively Nazi party was demanding that Austria be united with Germay, although this was expressly forbidden by the Versailles Treaty. They had made the same demand in 1934 and had murdered the Austrian Chancellor, Dollfuss. Then the opposition of Mussolini had prevented the *Anschluss*, or Union, of Austria with Germany taking place. Now however Mussolini was Hitler's ally, Britain and France would not take action. On 12 March 1938, German troops marched across the border. There was no resistance and soon Hitler was driving in triumph through the streets of Vienna to the applause of huge crowds. The *Anschluss* which bound the land of his birth to that of his adulthood was among the proudest moments of his life.

**Czechoslovakia 1938**  If the Germans were to expand into Eastern Europe they would have to take action against Czechoslovakia. At the western end of Czechoslovakia lay the Sudetenland which had been granted to the Czechs in 1919 to give them easily-defended borders and modern industry. However the majority of the Sudeten population was German-speaking and many of them wished to be part of Germany. Hitler was able to present himself as their champion and to point out that, according to the self-determination principle which had been used to decide the borders of Central and Eastern Europe in 1919, the Sudetenland ought justly be part of Germany. In the spring of 1938, Henlein, leader of the Sudeten Germans, began to campaign for greater freedom from Czech control and in September Hitler insisted that the Sudetenland be handed over to Germany. Thinking that they would have the support of Britain and France, the Czech government stood firm. They had a modern army and were ready to give a good account of themselves in the event of war.

Britain and France wavered however. Chamberlain, Britain's Prime Minister, did not believe that Czechoslovakia was worth a European war and busied himself searching for a *peaceful solution*. Finally in September 1938, Hitler for Germany, Mussolini for Italy, Chamberlain for Britain and Daladier for France met at **Munich**. There they agreed on the immediate hand-over of the Sudetenland to Germany. The Czechs, who had not been consulted and felt themselves betrayed, had no choice but to give in. Hitler had got just what he wanted and was convinced that Britain and France had no stomach to resist further German aggression. For his part, Chamberlain believed that his peaceful policies were triumphing, since Hitler gave him his word that Germany's ambitions in Europe were satisfied. 'I believe that it is peace in our time' he told a relieved British public on his return home. It was not.

### The Road to World War II 1938–9

In March 1939, German troops occupied all Czechoslovakia and, a few days later, the Lithuanian port of Memel. Then Hitler turned his attention on Poland. In Posen, the Polish Corridor, and Danzig there were millions of Germans. They and their lands he insisted, must be united with the Reich. Like the Czechs, the Poles stood fast and looked to Britain and France for support. Although in August Hitler had surprised the world by signing a non-aggression pact with Russia, his arch enemy (the Nazi–Soviet Pact), so making a German attack on Poland much less risky, **Britain and France were at last ready to fight**. The German occupation of all Czechoslovakia had convinced Chamberlain and British public opinion that **Hitler could not be trusted**. If Britain was ready to fight then France was too. Consequently, when the German army invaded Poland on 1 September 1939, World War II began.

### The Appeasement Policy of Britain and France

The word 'appeasement' is used to describe the policy of giving way to Hitler's demands in order to maintain the peace of Europe. Since we know that it failed and Europe suffered six dreadful years of war as a result of Hitler's aggression, it is easy to dismiss 'appeasement' as simple cowardice. This is not fair. Chamberlain, who was an experienced politician with a reputation for toughness in home affairs, had good reasons for this policy and British public opinion was for the most part fully behind him.

Both in Britain and France the experience of World War I had been so terrible that another war seemed unthinkable. There was great popular faith in the League of Nations, especially among the young. From 1933 to 1938 moreover Hitler's demands did not seem unreasonable. All he seemed to be asking was that the terms of the Versailles Treaty, which were harsh on Germany, should be ended and that the German minorities in Eastern Europe should have genuine self-determination. Right these wrongs, said Hitler, and Europe will have no reason to fear Germany. Chamberlain's mistake was to take Hitler at his word, but this was a mistake made by many experienced politicians both inside and outside Germany. Hitler was a master of deception and when he wanted could appear a statesman of sweet reason.

## The Main Events

| | |
|---|---|
| 1918 | World War I ends. The German *Kaiser* (Emperor) abdicates. |
| 1919 | Weimar Republic set up. Versailles Treaty signed. |
| 1919–23 | Political and economic confusion in Germany. |
| 1923 | French occupy the Ruhr. Extraordinary inflation. Nazis attempt to seize power in Munich (the Beer Hall *Putsch*). |
| 1923–4 | Hitler in the Landsberg prison. Writes *Mein Kampf*. |
| 1923–9 | Stresemann Chancellor, then Foreign Minister. |
| 1925 | Treaty of Locarno brings Germany on to better terms with former enemies. |
| 1926 | Germany admitted to the League of Nations. |
| 1929–33 | Wall Street Crash, more unemployment and more political extremism. |
| 1932 | Nazis the largest single party in the *Reichstag*. |
| 1933 | Hitler appointed Chancellor, *Reichstag* Fire. Enabling Acts. Germany leaves the League. |
| 1934 | Night of the Long Knives. Germany begins rearming. |
| 1935 | Anglo–German naval agreement. |
| 1935–6 | Italy attacks Abyssinia. |
| 1936 | Germans re-occupy the Rhineland. Rome–Berlin Axis established, anti-Comintern Pact with Japan. |
| 1936–9 | Spanish Civil War. |
| 1938 March | *Anschluss* with Austria. |
| September | Czechoslovak crisis. Munich agreement. |
| 1939 March | Germany occupies all Czechoslovakia, then Memel. |
| May | Pact of Steel with Italy. |
| August | Nazi–Soviet Pact. |
| September | German troops invade Poland. |

# Guide to Questions

There are two popular examination themes: the Nazis' Rise to Power and Hitler's Foreign Policy.

### Specimen Question 1

*Account for the rise of the Nazi Party in Germany up to 1933. How did Hitler establish his control over the German people before 1939?* (Cambridge 1979)

A two-part question. Allow yourself equal time for both parts. Remember that when you are asked to 'account for', you must respond with **reasons**. And when asked 'how', a relevant answer must concentrate on **methods**.

### Suggested essay plan

*1 Reasons* Stress two main reasons, the bitterness and despair of millions of Germans in the early 1930s and the skill with which the Nazis turned this bitterness to their own advantage. These general reasons can then be divided into more detailed particular ones. Start with a sentence like: 'The Nazi Party could not have won power in Germany in 1933 if in the early 1930s conditions within Germany had not been desperate. Millions of Germans viewed the immediate past with disgust and the future with dismay.' From such a beginning move directly to the particular causes of distress:

*a) Economic causes* The economic dislocations caused by the Versailles Settlement; problems with reparations; the occupation of the Ruhr and the catastrophic inflation of 1923; recovery 1924–9 but based on American loans; so the Wall Street Crash hits Germany specially hard. 6 million unemployed 1932.

*b) Political causes* The Weimar Republic was never strong between 1919 and 1933. A bad start in 1919 having to sign the Versailles Treaty. Both nationalists and Communists would have liked to overthrow it and the army felt no loyalty towards it. As a multi-party democracy most of its governments were coalitions and increasingly weak ones. Only prospered during Stresemann's years of office and he died in 1929.

*2 Nazi skill* Describe the skill of the Nazis in using this situation to their advantage as follows:

*a) The Nazi message* This was adapted to suit different groups. Anti-communism for the middle and upper classes; law and order and an aggressive foreign policy for the army officers; blame the Jews for the past and paint a proud and rosy future for the workers. To all Germans, continually criticize the Versailles Treaty.

*b) Nazi methods* Energetic campaigning and remarkable public speaking, Hitler especially. The private army of Brownshirts (the SA) to win the street battles. Magnificent ceremonial to give the image of power and purpose; Goebbels a master of propaganda. Complete lack of scruple; deceit and violence in constant use, e.g. the *Reichstag* Fire 1933. Ruthless and decisive use of their opportunities in 1933.

*3 Methods* The second part of the question asks how Hitler established control by 1939.

*a) By violence and fear of violence* Night of the Long Knives, purge of the army leadership 1938; threats, violence against property, concentration camps.

*b) Totalitarian controls* Censorship of newspapers, books and films. Control of the radio; indoctrination through education and youth movements. Banning of trades unions and all institutions which might challenge the Nazi bid for the hearts and minds of all Germans. Members of the armed forces bound by a personal oath of loyalty to the *Führer*.

*c) Loyalty won by successes*  Millions of Germans, both before and during the war, were ready to accept the control of the Nazis because they approved of what they could see of their actions. Up to 1942 Hitler was very successful. Unemployment falls fast after 1933, the national income rises equally fast. In foreign policy the Versailles Treaty successfully defied. Between 1933 and 1939 Hitler gave back to most Germans their hope and pride.

**Specimen Question 2**

*Study this Russian cartoon of 1936, and then answer questions (a) to (f) which follow:*

a)   Name (i) the 'baby' shown in the cradle; (ii) the two *capitalist powers shown on the left of the cartoon with hands on the cradle; (iii) the power which is represented by the figure smoking a cigar.*                                        *(4)*
b)   *What does the cartoonist's drawing of the 'baby' suggest about the regime over which the 'baby' presided?*                                        *(2)*
c)   *What, in your opinion, does the cartoonist suggest about the relationships at this time between the Western democracies and Nazi Germany?*                                        *(2)*
d)   *In what ways, before the publication of this cartoon, had Russian foreign policy responded to the birth of this 'baby'?*                                        *(3)*
e)   *In what year, and for what reason, did the Russian press suddenly cease to publish cartoons such as this?*                                        *(3)*
f)   *Explain the circumstances in which the 'baby' became involved in war with (i) the two figures on the left of the cartoon; (ii) the USSR; (iii) the figure smoking the cigar.*                                        *(6)*

(*Evidence in Question*, Watson, Rayner and Stapley)

An 'evidence' question. Note carefully the date and the distribution of marks per section. Attempt the answers on your own and then compare them with those on page 111.

# Chapter 12 *The Cold War 1945–51*

A month before World War II ended and a week before his own death, President Roosevelt of the USA wrote to Stalin of the USSR. 'It would be one of the greatest tragedies in history if at the very moment of victory now within our grasp, distrust and lack of faith should prejudice the entire undertaking after the colossal losses of life and material and treasure involved.' He felt that he had to write in such terms because the conference between the Allies, first at Teheran in 1943 and then at Yalta in 1945, had made little progress towards agreeing the main points of a future peace settlement. Communist Russia was deeply suspicious of the intentions of capitalist America and Britain and vice versa. Roosevelt's letter had no real effect. A further conference in 1945 at Potsdam did nothing to lessen these suspicions. Indeed so swiftly and bitterly did the former allies quarrel once Germany was defeated, that no grand peace settlement like those of Vienna or Versailles was possible.

## Allied Agreement

This is not to say that the victors of World War II disagreed about everything. In 1941, just before the USA entered the war, Roosevelt and Churchill met on board a warship and signed the so-called '*Atlantic Charter*'. This stated that neither the USA nor Britain would seek to increase their lands if they were victorious and that every nation should be free to make its own choice of government.

At Teheran in Iran in 1943 where Roosevelt, Churchill and Stalin met for the first time, they agreed that a new world organization should be established at the end of the war. Further discussions followed at Dumbarton Oaks in the USA in 1944 and, in 1945, in San Francisco, the *United Nations Organization* was successfully set up.

At Yalta in the Crimean region of the USSR, Roosevelt, Churchill and Stalin discussed the new boundaries for Europe. They agreed that *Germany should be divided* into Allied Occupation Zones and, in principle, about the *new Poland*. Russia was to take over a large slice of Eastern Poland while the Poles should be compensated in the west with a considerable addition of former German land. The new western border of Poland was provisionally fixed as the line of the Oder and Neisse rivers. This Oder–Neisse line was to cause great difficulties in the years to come, especially as there are two Neisse rivers running into the Oder!

At Potsdam near Berlin in 1945, Stalin represented Russia as usual but the new President Truman attended for the USA, and Churchill for Britain was replaced during the conference by Attlee, who had defeated him in the British General Election. Potsdam saw agreement on the form of the occupation of Germany. As well as the four Allied Occupation Zones (American, British, Russian and French), *Berlin*, the German capital, though deep inside the Russian Occupation Zone, was also to be divided into four sections, each with a Commander-in-Chief who would act together as the Control Council of the city. In each zone the occupying troops were to **disarm all Germans** and make clear to them their responsibility for the horrors of the war, to **bring war criminals to trial**, to destroy the Nazi Party in all its forms, to supervise the payment of **reparations** and to prepare the population for the eventual introduction of **democratic government**. At Nuremburg a special court was set up by the Allies, with the backing of the United Nations, to try twenty-one leading Nazis. Twelve were sentenced to death, six to long terms of imprisonment and the remaining three were acquitted.

Between 1945 and 1947, peace treaties were agreed with Germany's former allies—Italy, Hungary, Bulgaria and Romania. These treaties meant some **territorial changes**. Italy lost Venezia–Giulia and Fiume to Yugoslavia, while Trieste became a free city under the supervision of the United Nations. Hungary lost land to Czechoslovakia and Romania, who in turn lost land to Russia and to Bulgaria.

The Cold War: Europe after World War II

The last-named had to pay reparations. Finland lost Petsamo and other territory to Russia. Austria, like Germany, was divided into four zones of occupation, and Vienna, like Berlin well inside the Russian zone, was similarly split. In 1955 Austria achieved full independence when the occupying forces withdrew. However she was to remain neutral and was forbidden to unite with Germany.

## Disagreements

Yet disagreement between the victors greatly outweighed their agreement. Early in 1945 there were sharp differences of opinion, between Russia on the one hand and America and Britain on the other, concerning **reparations** and the **final boundaries of Poland**. In 1946 these differences were sharpened by the steps Russia was taking to make sure that she would dominate Eastern Europe. Though Britain in particular had agreed that Eastern Europe should be a Russian 'sphere of influence' both Britain and America had expected that **free elections** would take place and **democratic governments** along western lines appear. Russia's intention, however, was the creation of communist governments which would follow orders from Moscow. As the months passed the links between Eastern and Western Europe were broken and movement out of the Russian-controlled areas became difficult. Consequently in a famous speech in 1946 in Fulton, Missouri, Churchill declared that 'from Stettin on the Baltic to Trieste on the Adriatic an iron curtain was fallen across Europe. Behind that line lie all the ancient states of Central and Eastern Europe . . . This is certainly not the liberated Europe we fought to build up.' This '**iron curtain**' was a physical thing, sometimes barbed wire, minefields and watch-towers, sometimes concrete walls. Behind this formidable barrier, Russia worked away to bring to power governments absolutely loyal to her instructions. Her task was made easier by the fact that all Eastern Europe, with the exception of Yugoslavia, had been liberated by the Red Army and that army had not gone home.

## The Russian Take-over of Eastern Europe 1945–8

In **Poland** there was bitter rivalry between Mikolajczyck, leader of the Peasant Party (PSL), who had headed the Polish government in exile during the war and was anti-communist and the Polish Communist Party supported by Moscow. In the run-up to the 1947 elections, the PSL was terrorized and the Communists won a landslide victory. Mikolajczyck fled to London.

In **Bulgaria** there was a similar struggle between the non-communist Agrarian Party led by Petkov and the Communists. In the election of 1946 though the Agrarians were terrorized, Petkov claimed that they won 60 per cent of the vote. The official result, however, was an overwhelming victory for the Communists. The following year Petkov was tried for treason and executed.

When the Russians had occupied **Romania** in 1945, they had forced King Michael to appoint a Communist government. When elections were held in 1946, 200 opposition leaders were in prison and the communist printers' union refused to print any anti-communist election material. The Communists won a large majority. King Michael was forced to abdicate and Maniu, leader of the anti-communist

Peasant Party was sentenced to life imprisonment with hard labour.

Though **Hungary** was also occupied by the Red Army, genuinely free elections were held in November 1945. Then the non-communist Smallholders Party won 60 per cent of the vote against the Communists 17 per cent. The Russians insisted, however, that the ministries of the Interior and of Defence should be given to Communists who, in December 1946, declared that there were dangerous plots against the Hungarian people. They had many leading politicians arrested and forced the Prime Minister, Ferenc Nagy, to resign by threatening his family. In the elections that followed, the Communists won 90 per cent of the vote.

The **Czechoslovak** Communist Party was genuinely popular at the end of the war. In the elections of May 1946 it won 38 per cent of the vote and Gottwald, the Communist leader, shared power with non-communists, like Benes and Jan Masaryck. Between 1946 and 1948 Russian backing and massive communist trade-union demonstrations increased its power. In 1948, Masaryck either committed suicide or was murdered by a fall from an upper floor window and Benes resigned as President in favour of Gottwald.

In all these countries the triumphant Communist governments ended free elections, imposed censorship and obediently followed orders from Moscow. They are often described as Soviet '**satellites**' and the huge area of the world under Russian control as '**the Soviet bloc**'.

An important exception to this trend was **Yugoslavia**. Though it became Communist, it stayed independent of Moscow. This independence was possible because Yugoslavia had liberated herself from the Germans by her own efforts. Resistance had been led by Tito's communist Partisans and, in 1945 Tito had himself ruthlessly destroyed all opposition and set up his own one-party communist state. From 1945 to 1948, Tito and Stalin got on very well but then they fell out, especially when Tito made it clear that he intended to follow his own policies in the Balkans. Stalin tried to overthrow him by economic means and even thought of war. However Tito was a popular ruler and was also ready to turn to the West for support. Stalin decided to leave him alone but let loose a typically murderous purge of the leadership of the other Eastern European Communist parties to make sure that none of them would follow Tito's bad example.

**The Reaction of the West**

The West was most unhappy at these developments in Eastern Europe but, since the Red Army was in occupation, there was nothing to be done short of a major war, which no Western electorate was ready to consider. Events in **Greece** in 1946–7 caused a major crisis. Though Russia had agreed in 1945 that Greece should be a British 'sphere of influence', communist forces were winning a civil war there and Britain did not have the resources to continue to support the anti-communists. It seemed that there was no stopping the spread of communism. At this point, President Truman stepped in. 'It must be the policy of the US' he declared 'to support free peoples who are resisting attempted subjugation by armed minorities or by outside pressures.' He sent financial and military aid to the Greek anti-communists who eventually won the civil war.

This **Truman Doctrine** was followed by the **Marshall Plan**. General G. C. Marshall was Secretary of State (Foreign Minister) in Truman's government. In June 1947, he announced that the USA was offering economic aid to Europe on a vast scale. In the two years after the war, economic conditions throughout Europe had been appalling and the Americans feared that, unless there was an economic recovery, the spread of communism would continue. Nonetheless Marshall Aid was offered to Eastern as well as to Western Europe. Russia however was sure that it was 'an American design to enslave Europe' and forbade her satellites to have anything to do with it. On the contrary Stalin created two new organizations which even more clearly divided East from West. *Cominform* (1947) was to co-ordinate and extend Communist activities all over the world and *Comecon* (1949) was to bind Eastern Europe more closely to Russia economically, to counter-balance the tremendous success of Marshall Aid in the West.

### The Berlin Crisis 1948

So deep now was the distrust between the Communist East and the Capitalist West that the term 'Cold War' can accurately be used to describe their relationship. In 1948 there was nearly a hot war, the cause Berlin. The old German capital was well inside the Russian zone. Consequently the French, British and American sectors of the city were entirely surrounded by Russian-controlled territory. There was a disagreement over the reform of the German currency. The Western powers went ahead with the reform despite Russian objections. In retaliation the Russians *closed all surface communications* between Berlin and the West. Following the lead of the USA, the Western Powers agreed that they were not going to be bullied out of Berlin. By a continuous and expensive *airlift* they kept their sectors of Berlin supplied and made clear to the Russians that any interference with the supply planes would be regarded as an act of war. Eventually in 1949 the Russians re-opened the land routes out of Berlin. The Berlin airlift had kept West Berlin under Western control.

However the Cold War worsened. In 1949 the Western Powers (Belgium, Britain, the Netherlands, Luxemburg, Canada, Denmark, France, Ireland, Italy, Norway, Portugal and the USA) formed a military alliance, the *North Atlantic Treaty Organization* (NATO). Britain, France and the USA also *merged* their zones in 1949 and allowed the West Germans to elect a government. Adenauer became the first Chancellor of the *Federal German Republic* (FDR) which under his leadership became a major partner in the Western anti-communist alliance. The same year the Russian zone became the *German Democratic Republic* (DDR), with Grotewohl as its first Prime Minister. It was a one-party communist state, a major member of the Soviet bloc. In 1955, the FDR was allowed to rearm. In response Russia formed the *Warsaw Pact*, which co-ordinated all the military forces of the Communist bloc against NATO. Europe, and indeed the world, was split in two. The balance of power (or terror, since both sides were now armed with nuclear weapons) was very even.

## The Main Events

| | |
|---|---|
| 1941 | The Atlantic Charter (Roosevelt, Churchill). |
| 1943 | The Teheran Conference (Roosevelt, Churchill, Stalin). |
| 1945 February | The Yalta Conference (Roosevelt, Churchill, Stalin). |
| April–June | San Francisco Conference sets up the United Nations. |
| May | End of World War II in Europe. |

| July | Potsdam Conference (Truman, Churchill then Attlee, Stalin). |
| 1945–8 | Soviet take-over of Eastern Europe. |
| 1946–7 | Greek Civil War. |
| 1947 | Truman Doctrine, Marshall Aid. |
| 1948 | Tito and Stalin quarrel. |
| 1948–9 | Berlin Crisis and airlift. |
| 1949 | The two halves of Germany become separate states. NATO set up, Comecon too. |

**Later developments in the Soviet bloc**   1953 Disturbances in East Germany put down by Russian troops.   1955 Warsaw Pact signed.   1956 Hungarian revolt against Russian domination crushed by Russian tanks; Nagy, the Hungarian leader, taken to Russia and eventually executed.   1968 Czechoslovak rising against Russian domination put down by Warsaw Pact forces; Dubcek, the Czechoslovak leader, disgraced.


## Guide to Questions


### Specimen Question 1

*'He won a large popular following as a resistance leader during World War II and ruled the country after the war. Although a convinced Communist, he was in no hurry to collectivize agriculture, preferring peasant small-holdings. He received loans from the IMF and made his independent links with the Third World. These polices were very unpopular in Moscow. Nevertheless he remained firmly in power in spite of Russian reprisals'.*

This extract describes:   A *Horthy in Hungary*    D *Tito in Yugoslavia*
   B *Hoxha in Albania*    E *Ulbricht in East Germany*
   C *Papandreou in Greece*

(*New Objective Tests in Twentieth Century History*, Rayner, Stapley and Watson.)

If you are not sure of the answer, don't guess. Try to get there by a process of elimination. Horthy was a Hungarian conservative who held power between the wars so it cannot be A. Hoxha of Albania began by being very loyal to Stalin and then switched to support Communist China. He would never accept loans from the International Monetary Fund and kept Albania isolated from the rest of the world, so it cannot be B. Nor can it be C since Papandreou was a Greek Socialist not a Communist, nor E since Ulbricht was always loyal to Moscow. So it must be D, Tito in Yugoslavia.


### Specimen Question 2

*The Truman Doctrine of 1947 was intended to counter an attempted take-over of*
A *Czechoslovakia*    D *Greece*
B *Finland*    E *Italy*
C *Egypt*
(*New Objective Tests in Twentieth Century History*, Rayner, Stapley and Watson.)

It cannot be A since Czechoslovakia had to a large extent been taken over by the Communists in 1947. Nor can it be Finland which in 1947 had a Communist government, which was in fact to be voted out of office the following year. Since neither Italy nor Egypt were seriously threatened by an attempted Communist takeover (C and E) it must be D, Greece, where in fact the Communists were winning the Civil War.

## Specimen Question 3

*What is meant by the 'Cold War'? Who was involved in it? Describe two events which were a manifestation of the Cold War.* (AEB, 1979)

A word of warning. Twentieth Century syllabusses come to an end at different times. The Cold War began in 1945 and was still continuing, though in a changed form, at the time of writing this book. (1982) So where you should end your account of the Cold War will depend to some extent on the syllabus which you are taking. This AEB question is from a syllabus which ends in 1951. If you are taking a similar syllabus, make clear to the examiner in your answer that the Cold War was not limited to Europe nor to the late forties and early fifties but draw your example from Europe before 1951.

### Suggested essay plan

*1 What is meant by the Cold War?* The condition of extreme suspicion and hostility which developed, between the Communist 'bloc' led by Russia and the capitalist 'bloc' headed by the USA, in the years immediately after World War II. Though a full scale 'hot' war has threatened, it has not yet become a reality.

*2 Who was involved in it?* On the Communist side, Russia and her satellites in Eastern Europe: Poland, East Germany (the Democratic Republic of Germany), Czechoslovakia, Hungary, Romania and Bulgaria. Also in the 1950s Communist China and Albania. In the 1960s, however, a rift developed between Russia and China. The Soviet bloc was bound militarily by the Warsaw Pact (1955) and economically by Comecon (1949). On the capitalist side were the USA and the powers of Western Europe and North America represented in the North Atlantic Treaty Organization, i.e. Canada, Britain, France, Benelux, Italy, Portugal and West Germany (the Federal Republic of Germany). Within Europe, the Scandinavian countries, Spain, Austria, Switzerland and Yugoslavia stayed neutral. Western European nations were linked economically by Marshall Aid.

*3 Two events which were manifestations (signs) of the Cold War*

*a) Greece 1946–7* a communist versus anti-communist civil war; Greece agreed by Stalin and Churchill to be a British 'sphere of influence', an exhausted Britain unable to keep supporting anti-communists. A communist victory seems likely. President Truman of the USA worried by the recent take-over of Eastern Europe by Communists is ready to take Britain's place. States 'The Truman Doctrine' whereby America promises to come to the aid of any free people threatened by a minority take-over or outside attacks. American money and military aid sent to Greece. Anti-communists win.

*b) Berlin 1948–9* West Berlin a capitalist 'Western' oasis surrounded by a Communist desert. Currency crisis causes Russia to cut all surface communications with the West. Western powers do not give in. Airlift supplies into West Berlin. War seems very close. Airlift successful since the Russians eventually re-open surface links in 1949. But relations between major powers further damaged. Western powers form NATO in 1949. Soviet bloc sets up Cominform then Comecon and Warsaw Pact.

# Further Questions

*1* Explain the policies of Metternich with regard to:
  a) the Congress of Aix-la-Chapelle 1818
  b) the Carlsbad Decrees 1819
  c) the Congress of Troppau 1820
  d) the Congress of Verona 1822. (Cambridge, 1976)

*2* What were the terms of the Treaty of Vienna (1815) for (a) France (b) Poland and (c) the Italian States? What were the consequences of the settlement for these countries over the next 15 years? (AEB, 1979)

*3* How did the Greeks achieve independence? (AEB, 1979)

*4* The invasion of the Crimea by British and French armies was intended to:
  a) force Russian troops to leave the Danubian principalities
  b) restore Turkish power in Constantinople
  c) reverse the terms of the Treaty of Unkiar–Skelessi
  d) destroy the naval base at Sebastopol. (Cambridge, 1978)

*5* 'The year 1848 was a year of revolutions.' Explain why revolutions occurred (a) in France and (b) in the territories ruled by the Habsburgs. Account for the immediate success of the revolutionaries in France and the ultimate failure of the revolutionaries in the Habsburg Empire. (London, 1976)

*6* Account for the failure of the attempt to unite Italy in 1848–9 and for the success of the attempt in the years 1858–61. (AEB, 1979)

*7* Describe the political situation in France in 1848 between February and October and explain how the situation enabled Louis Napoleon to acquire power that year. (Oxford, 1976)

*8* What do you think were Napoleon III's three greatest successes and three greatest failures before 1870? Give reasons for your choice. (AEB, 1979)

*9* To what extent was the cause of Italian unity furthered by (a) Mazzini (b) Cavour and (c) Garibaldi? (Oxford, 1977)

*10* What obstacles stood in the way of a united Italy? How far had they been overcome by 1861? (Oxford and Cambridge, 1979)

*11* How was Germany united between 1863 and 1871? (Cambridge, 1978)

*12* Explain the importance for Prussia of 3 of the following: (a) the Treaty of Olmutz (b) the Prussian Constitution of 1850, (c) the Convention of Gastein (d) the Ems Telegram. (Oxford, 1977)

*13* Study the photograph (opposite) of a meeting in a Russian village in the period after 1861, and then answer questions (a) to (f) which follow:
  a) To what class did the people of this meeting belong?     *(1)*
  b) Name the institution represented by a meeting such as this, and explain the role which was given to this institution by a decree published in 1861 by Alexander II.     *(3)*

c) What evidence does this photograph provide concerning life in a Russian village at this time? You should pay particular attention in your answer to the standard of living, and to the level of education. *(4)*

d) Suggest reasons why it was likely to have been difficult in the 1860s for those shown in this photograph to leave their village. *(3)*

e) In what other institution, created by Alexander II, would these Russians have been represented in the 1860s and 1870s, and to what extent would they still have been represented in it by the end of the century? *(3)*

f) Why were Russians such as these often discontented in the years 1861 to 1917? *(6)*

*(Evidence in Question,* Watson, Rayner and Stapley)

**14** Explain the causes of the Russo–Japanese War of 1904–5. What were the consequences of the war with Russia? (Oxford and Cambridge, 1979)

**15** Identify and explain the main reasons why each of the following countries became involved in the war of 1914: Austria–Hungary, France, Germany, Russia, Serbia. Which of these countries do you consider was most to blame for the outbreak of the European War? (London, 1976)

**16** In what ways were international relations affected by the policies of Kaiser Wilhelm (William) II between 1890 and 1910 (Oxford, 1977)

**17** Why was there growing unrest during the reign of Nicholas II? Describe the main features of the revolutions of 1917. (JMB, 1976)

**18** 'From 1917 to 1939 Russia had three revolutions: one which overthrew the Tsar, one which brought the Bolsheviks to power and one which produced an economic transformation.' Describe each of these revolutions and explain which, in your opinion, was most beneficial to Russia. (London, 1976)

**19** a) Examine the map 'Europe after 1918' (on page 104), and then answer the following:
(i) name City A; (ii) which country owned City B before 1914?; (iii) name City B;

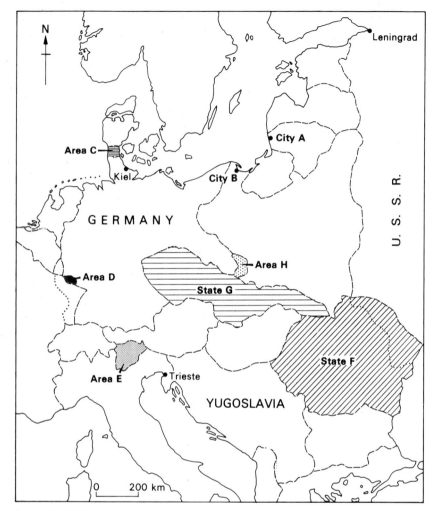

Europe after 1918

(iv) how did the Powers protect the German population in City B?; (v) name Area C; (vi) to which country did Area C belong after July 1920?; (vii) name Area D; (viii) who administered Area D from 1919 to 1935?; (ix) name Area E; (x) who gained Area E in 1919?; (xi) name State F; (xii) name State G; (xiii) name Area H; (xiv) why was the ownership of Area H in dispute in 1919? *(14)*

b) Describe the main territorial changes which broke up the Empire of Austria–Hungary after the First World War. (JMB, 1975) *(6)*

**20** Explain the importance, for the League of Nations, of the following crises: (i) Corfu 1923–4, (ii) Manchuria 1931–3, (iii) Abyssinia 1935–6. (Oxford, 1975)

**21** Write an account of the foreign policy of Adolf Hitler between 1933 and 1939. Explain the attitudes of the British and French governments to this policy (Cambridge, 1979)

**22** Hitler's extermination of the SA was intended to strengthen his support from the German A army
        B Gestapo
        C industrialists
        D middle class
        E socialists.

**23** 'Europe after World War II was dominated by the German problem.' Show how Germany was treated after World War II and explain what you understand by the German problem. What developments had taken place in Germany by 1951 and how did these affect the relationships of the Great Powers? (London, 1976)

**24** Explain the circumstances which led to three of the following, showing the importance of each in the development of the Cold War: (a) the partition of Germany; (b) Churchill's Fulton speech; (c) the Marshall Plan; (d) the Communist coup in Czechoslovakia, 1948; and (e) the Berlin blockade 1948–9. (Oxford, 1977)

# Answers

### Chapter 1 Specimen Question 1

a) The German Confederation.

b) (i) The Austrian or Habsburg Empire; (ii) Francis II; (iii) Metternich; (iv) Vienna.

c) (i) Lombardy and Venetia respectively; (ii) the Quadrilateral.

d) F for France and H for Spain are the only two nation-states lettered on the map. N.B. a nation-state is a country with clear boundaries the majority of whose population shares a common language and a common history.

e) Alexander I of Russia took charge of Area E, Poland. Though he granted the Poles a constitution, he made sure that they remained under Russian control.

f) Area B, the former Austrian Netherlands and Holland were united under the Dutch king to act as a buffer along the northern border of France.

g) CD is Prussia. The Prussians did well out of the peace settlement of 1814–15. Though they gave up part of Poland and failed to gain as much of Saxony as they had hoped, they made large gains in the Rhineland provinces. This expansion of Prussian power in the west was of great importance in the later struggle with Austria for supremacy within Germany. It came about partly because the Prussian army had played a major part in the defeat of Napoleon, partly to make sure that there was a strong buffer state on the eastern border of France, and partly so that the major powers of Europe were in balance.

### Chapter 2 Specimen Question 1

a) (i) Port A is Varna, Port B Evpatoria, Battle C Sinope, Town D Scutari, River E the Alma, Territory F Moldavia–Wallachia.

(ii) Russia claimed the right to protect all Christians within the Turkish Empire.

b) (i) Territory F (Moldavia–Wallachia) was to remain part of the Turkish Empire but to have greater self-government.

No warships were to enter the Black Sea in times of peace.

The River Danube became an international waterway.

(ii) Piedmont (Sardinia) contributed to the Allied victory and was represented at the Paris conference.

(iii) The peace settlement lasted so short a time (a) because it was too hard on Russia who consequently was determined to threaten Turkey once again as soon as she had recovered from her defeat; and (b) because it did nothing to solve the problems in the Balkans. Since the Turks proved unwilling or unable to carry out their promised reforms, the situation in the Balkans grew more dangerous.

### Chapter 5 Specimen Question 1

i) River X is the Po, City Y Venice and City Z Palermo.

ii) (a) Region B (Lombardy) was united to Region A (Piedmont–Sardinia) in 1859. This union was the direct result of the French invasion of Northern Italy in support of the Piedmontese. Napoleon III and Cavour had planned this at Plombières in 1858. Cavour was to provoke the Austrians to war. The French army would defeat the Austrians. Piedmont would make gains in Northern Italy and give France in return Nice and Savoy. This plan was put into effect in 1859. The French won the battles of Magenta and Solferino. Though Napoleon III decided to end the war and signed the Truce of Villafranca with the Austrians without consulting the Piedmontese, he had done enough to win them Lombardy.

(b) Region C (the Kingdom of the Two Sicilies ruled by the Bourbon king Francis II) was united to Regions A and B in 1860. How? Mainly through the heroism of Garibaldi and the Thousand who sailed from Genoa, landed in Sicily, won the battle of Calatafimi, occupied Palermo and then invaded the mainland of Southern Italy. As they advanced on Naples, popular revolts further weakened the power of Francis II. Garibaldi quickly captured Naples and Victor Emmanuel, King of Piedmont, then marched south with the Piedmontese army. He and Cavour were worried lest Southern Italy should be reorganized by Garibaldi, independent of Piedmont. They also feared that Garibaldi might gain the enmity of the Great Powers by trying to take Rome from the Pope. Garibaldi handed over his conquests to Victor Emmanuel and the inhabitants of Southern Italy then voted overwhelmingly, by plebiscite, to be united with Piedmont.

iii) Region D is the Papal States. (N.B. you are *not* asked when and how it was united to the rest of Italy, you are asked what *special difficulties* its acquisition presented.) The special difficulties arose from the fact that the Pope was the head of the Roman Catholic Church with millions of followers throughout Europe. And Pius IX was strongly opposed to giving way to the nationalists by handing over his territories to them. He could count on Austrian support and was defended in Rome by French troops.

### Chapter 5 Specimen Question 2

a) (i) The Neo-Guelphs most favoured a federal solution and they wanted the Pope as its leader.
   (ii) A federation is an association of states which accept a common leader and constitution but which keep to themselves considerable freedom of action (e.g. the USA).
   (iii) Mazzini was the most famous Italian leader who supported an Italian Republic.
b) 1849 (*not* 1848).
c) France and Austria.
d) Because in order to get Austria out of Italy, Cavour had sought French aid; because the attempted assassination of Napoleon III by Orsini in 1858 made Napoleon III more ready to help the cause of Italian unity; because Napoleon III had agreed in 1858 at Plombières that if Cavour was able to provoke a war with Austria France would come to Piedmont's aid and, in 1859, Cavour did succeed in provoking such a war.
e) The main obstacles to Italian unification after 1859 were the Bourbons in Southern Italy, the Austrians who still ruled Venetia and Pope Pius IX who still ruled the Papal States and the city of Rome.
f) In 1860 Garibaldi invaded Sicily with his thousand volunteers. After successfully liberating the island from the Bourbons he crossed to the mainland and reached Naples. The Piedmontese army marched south to meet him, defeating a Papal army

on the way. Garibaldi handed his conquests over to the Piedmontese and all the territories voted by plebiscite for union with Piedmont. This left Venetia under Austrian control and Rome, held for the Pope by a French army. In 1866, Italy sided with the Prussians during their war against Austria and received Venetia as a consequence of the Prussian victory. In 1870, the Franco-Prussian War caused the French troops to leave Rome. The Italians immediately took possession of the city and made it their capital. [Resist the temptation to write out all you know about Italian Unification in answer to (f). It states 'trace briefly' and means what it says since only 6 out of 20 marks are allocated to it.]

## Chapter 6  Specimen Question 1

a) Prussia (N.B. the seated figure is King William I not Bismarck who did not possess such bushy whiskers!)

b) (i) The Franco–Prussian War.
   (ii) King William I of Prussia.

c) (i) In the previous few months French armies had been badly defeated by the Prussians. Marshal Bazaine had taken refuge in Metz, Marshal MacMahon and the Emperor Napoleon III surrendered at Sedan. The Prussian armies therefore had been able to advance on Paris and the king to set up his headquarters at Versailles.
   (ii) The significance of the map lies in the fact that though the Emperor had been totally defeated (and had in fact abdicated) and there was no army left to defend them, the Parisians fought on. King William is studying the map in order to decide how to make the Prussian siege of Paris most effective.
   (iii) The point the cartoonist is making in his reference to the ghostly conversation is that in the time of the two ghosts (Napoleon I on the left and Louis XIV on the right) France was the most powerful military nation in Europe, unlike 1870, and won many glorious victories.

d) Napoleon III. He had been declared deposed by the Parisians after his defeat at Sedan and lived until his death in England.

e) (i) In the Crimea, the French army fought the best of the various armies involved. Victory over the Russians was achieved and, at the peace negotiations which were held in Paris in 1856, France gained prestige. The ghosts would have approved.
   (ii) They would not however have approved of the Mexican adventure. Napoleon III rashly sent troops to assist Maximilian against the Mexican rebels and then withdrew them leaving Maximilian in the lurch. The latter fought on but was eventually captured and executed. France appeared to have behaved most dishonourably.

f) The Franco–Prussian War marked a major change in the balance of power in Europe. Previously France, Austria, Prussia and Russia had been more or less in balance and this balance had been an important reason why Europe remained at peace between 1815 and 1854. The events of 1870–1 following Prussia's victory over Austria in 1866 created a German Empire which was much stronger than any one of the other 'Great Powers'. Furthermore this Empire was expanding economically at a rapid rate and increased rather than lessened as a threat in the eyes of her neighbours.

## Chapter 7 Specimen Question 1

a) (i) Nicholas II.

(ii) Nicholas I.

b) The Orthodox Church; the Jews suffered most from religious persecutions.

c) Lawful guarantees = to be able to use the law-courts to prevent the government's secret police locking up anyone they felt like.

Secret police = special police like members of the Third Section who were employed secretly by the government to spy upon possible opponents.

Fatricidal blood = the blood spilt by the struggle of brother against brother, of Russian against Russian, in other words the terrorism and counter-terrorism which had been growing in Russia since the 1870s.

100 million souls = the peasant farmers of Russia.

d) Tolstoy made special mention of the industrial workers because in the growing industrial cities they were becoming increasingly involved in anti-government movements. They were *now* significant because rapid industrialization in the 1890s had greatly increased their numbers and new parties like Plekhanov's Marxist Social Democrats were aiming to make them revolutionary.

e) Either (i) where an outline of the domestic reforms of Alexander II is needed (see page 54).

Or (ii) where the events and causes of the revolution of 1905 is required (see pages 55–6).

## Chapter 8 Specimen Question 1

a) Province A is Bosnia. The international crisis surrounding it in 1908 arose because Austria annexed it. Previously, since 1878, it had been administered by Austria but was legally still part of the Turkish Empire. Both Russia and Serbia opposed the annexation; the Russians felt that the Austrians had double-crossed them, Serbia believed that Bosnia was rightfully hers. Since Germany backed Austria, Russia and Serbia had to accept the Austrian annexation for the time being. However the crisis of 1908 increased hostilities in the Balkans.

b) D, E and F are respectively Serbia, Bulgaria and Romania. In the first Balkan War, Serbia, Bulgaria, Greece and Montenegro attacked and defeated the Turks, driving them back almost to the walls of Constantinople. In the second, 1913, Bulgaria, disappointed by her gains in 1912, attacked Serbia, who was supported by Greece, Montenegro, Romania and Turkey. Bulgaria was completely defeated. At the end of these wars, Serbia, who had gained in each was very confident and ready for war with Austria. Bulgaria was bitter because of her losses in 1913 and ready to turn to Austria and Germany as allies rather than Russia. Romania had mixed feelings. She had made gains at the expense of Bulgaria but was unhappy at the success of Serbia.

c) C is Albania. It was created in 1912 on the insistence of the Great Powers, partly to satisfy the demand of the Albanians for independence and partly to prevent Serbia from gaining a foothold on the Adriatic coast.

d) Town B is Sarajevo in Bosnia. There in June 1914, Archduke Ferdinand, heir to the Austrian throne, was assassinated by Bosnian nationalists. The immediate consequence of the murder was a tough ultimatum from Austria to Serbia whose secret service had helped the assassins. When Serbia was unable to agree to all the terms of the ultimatum, Austria, backed by Germany, declared war on Serbia. When Russia ordered a general mobilization, Germany declared war on Russia and, putting the Schlieffen Plan into effect, attacked France through Belgium. Britain then declared war on Germany. Thus in hardly more than a month, the assassination of the Archduke Ferdinand had led to the outbreak of World War I.

### Chapter 9  Specimen Question 2

a) (i) Russia (the USSR).
   (ii) Hitler.
b) Marx with Engels was the founder of Communism which looked forward to creating a world of equality, peace and co-operation once the workers had won power by a successful revolution. The standing man is puzzled since Marx did not predict a violent individual dictator like Stalin.
c) The purges from 1935–9 of leading members of the Communist Party and army and the revised constitution of 1936.
d) (i) The Nazi–Soviet Pact of 1939 united Hitler and Stalin. (ii) This agreement was shattered by the German invasion of Russia in 1941.
e) The comparison was appropriate in many ways: both Hitler and Stalin were power-mad and violent dictators who aimed through terror to control the lives of their subjects; both were determined to build up the power of their nations as rapidly as possible whatever the cost in individual suffering; the main difference between them was that Stalin concentrated on economic, Hitler on foreign policy.

### Chapter 10  Specimen Question 1

a) Wilson's war aims are usually known as the Fourteen Points.
b) The reference to Belgium comes first because Germany's invasion of Belgium in 1914 was the immediate cause of Britain going to war.
c) During the war Serbia had been over-run by Austria and Bulgaria. After the victory of 1918 she was united with Bosnia, Herzegovina, Montenegro and Dalmatia to form the new kingdom of Yugoslavia.
d) Alsace and Lorraine were the provinces lost to Germany in 1871 following France's defeat in the Franco–Prussian War. They were returned to France in 1919.
e) In the extract the word 'reparation' is used rather vaguely, 'reparations for injustice done'. During the peace negotiations it became much more precise and referred to the money which the defeated would have to pay to the victors to repair the damage done by the war. This sum was eventually fixed at £6,600,000.
f) Poland gained Posen, part of Upper Silesia and the Polish Corridor from Germany. Danzig, formerly a German port and inhabited by both Germans and Poles became a free city. The Germans disliked these decisions for two main reasons. The Polish Corridor divided East Prussia from the rest of Germany and millions of Germans passed under Polish rule without having the right of self-determination which the Settlement allowed to the other peoples of Europe.
g) Lloyd George's principles for the future of Austria–Hungary for the most part became a reality after the war. Genuine self-government on democratic principles came to the South Slavs in their new Yugoslav nation, to the Czechs and Slovaks in Czechoslovakia and to the Poles in Poland. Hungary, though it lost most of its Romanian-inhabited provinces to Romania, became completely independent. It cannot be said however that democratic governments flourished in Eastern Europe between the wars nor that the many minority groups within these new nations felt themselves fairly treated.